PARADES!

PARADES!

Celebrations and Circuses on the March

Gary Jennings

J. B. Lippincott Company

PHILADELPHIA   NEW YORK

for Fran and Herman Begega
compañeros de mi vida

ACKNOWLEDGMENTS

For his brief personal experience as an active parader, the author is indebted (if that's the word) to Company I of the 39th Infantry Regiment, 9th Infantry Division, U. S. Army. For more recent assistance in the preparation of this book—information, advice, and in many cases the loan of valuable photographs—the author owes sincere gratitude and thanks to the following individuals, companies, institutions, and government bureaus:

Miriam Abramowicz, Belgian Government Information Center.

M. Antipov, First Secretary, Permanent Mission of the U.S.S.R. to the United Nations.

John G. Baker of Barkin, Herman & Associates, Milwaukee, Wisconsin.

Anne Bastian, Consular Assistant, Luxembourg Consulate General.

V. Bogachev, Press Department, Embassy of the Union of Soviet Socialist Republics.

Marge Booker, San Francisco (Cal.) Convention and Visitors Bureau.

The British Travel Association.

Kaj Bruun, Press Attaché, Danish Information Office.

Paulo Guilherme V. B. Castro, Deputy Consul of Brazil.

Mia Chaplin, British Information Services.

Vivia Chow, Secretary, Consulate General of the Republic of China.

Jan H. Daman, Netherlands Information Office.

Jorge G. Dias, Tourist and Information Services, Casa de Portugal.

German Information Center.

Uno Gronkvist, Assistant Director, Swedish National Travel Office.

Matti Hakkanen, Vice-Consul of Finland.

Kurt Hampe, Director, Austrian Information Service.

Lt. Col. Hal H. Harlan, U. S. Air Force.

Walter B. Hoover, Chamber of Commerce of the New Orleans (La.) Area.

S. Irtiza Husain, Consul-General of Pakistan.

Institut Grand Ducal, Luxembourg

Istituto Italiano di Cultura.

Italian State Tourist Office.

Ernst Jaakson, Consul of Estonia.

Miss Romana Javitz, Curator, Picture Collection, New York Public Library.

Miss Kendal Kelly, Columbia Festivals, Inc., New York, N. Y.

Korean Research and Information Service, Embassy of Korea.

Luis Lopez-Ballesteros, Information Counselor, Embassy of Spain.

Joseph Lustenberger, Vice-Consul of Switzerland.

Dick MacMillan, Hawaii Visitors Bureau.

Nicholine Mellish, Information Bureau, Royal Afghan Embassy.

Mexican Government Tourism Department.

A. M. Moussa, General Manager, Tourist Offices Department, United Arab Republic.

Mrs. L. S. Nadhan, Assistant Director, Government of India Tourist Office.

Naval Historical Foundation, U.S. Navy Department.

Robert L. Parkinson, Superintendent of Historic Collections, Circus World Museum, Baraboo, Wisconsin.

Pasadena (Cal.) Tournament of Roses Association.

I. Pilosoph, Israel Information Service.

Monique Polgar, Assistant Director, Service de Presse et d'Information, Embassy of France.

Miss Elizabeth Roth, Curator, Print Room, New York Public Library.

Mirko Sardelic, Savezni Sekretarijat za Informacije, Yugoslavia.

Mrs. E. Satiropoulos, Press and Information Service, Royal Greek Embassy.

Jos. Schlitz Brewing Company, Milwaukee, Wisconsin.

M. Fouad Shadi, Director, United Arab Republic Tourist and Information Center.

Mike Shapiro, 20th Century-Fox Film Corporation, New York, N. Y.

South African Information Service.

Lt. Cmdr. J. C. Standiford, U.S. Navy

Patricia Stickler, Philadelphia (Pa.) Convention and Tourist Bureau.

John Swift, Vice-Consul of Ireland.

Yoshio Tagaya, Director, Japan National Tourist Organization.

The U. S. Army, Office of the Chief of Information.

D.C. Welden, Calgary (Alberta, Canada) Exhibition and Stampede.

Pierre Wurth, Consul of Luxembourg.

And a specially deep bow to Mrs. Emma Alden Rothblatt, First Deputy Commissioner, Department of Public Events, New York City.

Contents

PARADES!

I

"Is It Serious or Is It for Fun?"

ONE DAY NOT LONG AGO, a young French girl visiting New York City watched a parade of oddly-costumed men march up Fifth Avenue. Half amused and half puzzled, she turned to an American friend and said, "It is very curious, no? Explain to me, is it serious or is it for fun?"

On this occasion, the parade was strictly for fun. A men's society called the International Order of the Alhambra was holding a convention in New York at the time, and its members decided to put on a show for the city folk by marching up the avenue dressed in Moorish regalia—colored fezzes, false beards, bright sashes, baggy pantaloons, and curly-toed slippers.

But that wondering girl's question could be asked about every parade that has ever marched—"Is it serious or is it for fun?"—and in some cases it would be difficult for a watcher to say which. If he is seeing a particular parade for the first time, he may not know whether he's expected to cheer, laugh, doff his hat in salute, or bow his head in reverence.

For example, to an American tourist the traditional Spanish procession called The Funeral of the Sardine might well seem "very curious, no?"—a whole parade devoted to carrying a sardine through the streets, then burying it in a wee paper coffin. Though it may look comical to an outsider, this is actually a solemn religious ritual, signifying that the people are going to give up their favorite foods, treats, and luxuries during the holy season of Lent.

No parade marches in a vacuum. That is to say, it always has *some* reason for being. And often the parade is just a part of some additional

GAY, GAUDY, AND GLAMOROUS, *the circus parade is probably the best-known and best-loved of all street processions.*

ceremony or entertainment. A circus parade is merely a preview of the circus performance. An elaborate religious procession may lead worshippers to an even more elaborate church service. A public parade may open a holiday, but then the marchers will disperse to spend most of the day feasting and having fun in the privacy of their homes. So, to help you better understand and enjoy all sorts of parades, this book will occasionally direct your attention to what goes on before and after the marching.

While a parade may be sportive or serious, there is one thing it can't be—and that is modest. There is no such thing as a *bashful* parade. Whatever its reason for being, it is intended to draw a crowd, and almost always does. Just about everybody loves a parade, and there is not a single human community on earth which does not hold one sort or another.

In addition to being generally enjoyable, parades have also served practical purposes. Until only about a hundred and fifty years ago, the mass of people in the world were unable to read, but their parades provided a handy substitute for history books. The yearly celebration of their country's discovery or founding, its battle victories and heroes, kept them aware of their national heritage, and proud of it. Similarly, the parades held on holy days kept them reminded of their religion's history and beliefs, and of their own religious obligations.

To this day, parades provide what might be called a "world history in highlights." They mark the milestones of human progress; as when a heroic astronaut is honored with a triumphal parade. And they record some of history's saddest moments, too—after all, any parade that celebrates some army's victory also marks another's defeat. The make-up of any parade tells us something about the paraders' customs and tastes in music, color, art, costume, modes of transportation—even, in the design of the floats, their architecture. A parade may record the customs of a bygone day, as well; the marchers in a Columbus Day parade, for instance, often give us a look at the costumes of the fifteenth century.

Besides recording history, parades can sometimes help make it. Though not very showy, the "picket line" is one sort of parade that has done so. Since the 1800's, workers have used this tactic—leaving their jobs and marching up and down in front of their employer's place of business—to demand better wages or better working conditions. The picket line has usually achieved its aims, and the workers' increased prosperity and dignity have caused far-reaching changes in the world's ways of life.

CUSTOMS AND COSTUMES *of an earlier day are often re-created in a modern procession. These Japanese paraders wear the garb of nobles and warriors of five centuries ago.*
(JAPAN NATL. TOURIST ASSN.)

A TYPICAL PICKET LINE *of the 1930's. The marchers are employees of a New Jersey plant, on strike to demand better wages and working conditions.*

A similar sort of parade, the "demonstration march," has become increasingly frequent over the past few years. This is a parade of people who are all in favor of—or in protest against—some change in government policy, in the current set of laws, or just in the way their fellow men behave. Various parades have marched to demand the junking of nuclear weapons, to complain about the unfair treatment of Negroes and other minority groups, to plead for an end to war, etc. These parades don't offer much in the way of spectacle or entertainment. Indeed, they are often resented—even booed or stoned—by the spectators. But they do make their point: that a goodly number of people are "in step" and in agreement on whatever the cause may be.

It must be admitted that the motive behind some parades is not always praiseworthy. Throughout history, the tyrant or the dictator has employed the drama and excitement of parades to hypnotize his unhappy subjects into loyal followers, or to stir them into a warlike frenzy for his own base purposes. Many a victory parade is less a celebration than a cruel gloating over the vanquished. A military parade may be a threatening gesture toward other nations. A community may arrange a gala parade for no other purpose than to enrich the local merchants by attracting free-spending tourists. And in these pages

A TYPICAL DEMONSTRATION MARCH *of the 1960's. Negro and white students parade to protest the "segregation" policies of the New York City school system.*

you'll review other parades that have had even more ignoble reasons for marching.

We tend to think of parades as once-in-a-while events. But actually they are so frequent and common in our society today that *you,* no matter how shy and retiring you may be, will almost certainly march in one or more of them during your lifetime. Boy Scouts, Girl Scouts, many other organizations of young people often parade on their own or take part in adults' parades. Boys who enter military service, of course, can expect parading to be a part of it. But, boy or girl, you will most likely march in an academic cap-and-gown procession to mark your graduation from high school or college. And, boy or girl, the odds are that you will eventually march in at least one "indoor parade"—your wedding procession up a church aisle.

THE ACADEMIC PROCESSION. *In this graduation parade at the University of Helsinki, Finland, the young men and women are formally dressed and wear circlets of laurel leaves on their heads.*

THE WEDDING PROCESSION, *but hardly a typical one. This is the traditional military wedding, where the bride and bridegroom parade out of the chapel beneath an arch of sabers held by the young man's fellow officers.*

We have no way of knowing when the very first of all parades took place, but we can make a guess that probably comes close to the truth. The guess is that the first parade occurred sometime back in the dim, distant Stone Age, with the homecoming of a band of cavemen after a successful hunting expedition. We can imagine them trooping home, holding high the carcass of a slain deer or boar, and chanting and thumping their chests in pride. The first parade-watchers would have been the stay-at-home women, children, and old folks, who would come running to greet the returning hunters, to applaud their prowess and yell hooray at the prospect of a banquet.

Of course, these crude and savage people wouldn't have realized that they were holding what we'd call a "triumphal procession." But they must have found it a satisfying thing to do. The hunters would naturally enjoy being the heroes of the moment, and their welcoming families would take pleasure in making that moment a noisy and exciting one.

In some ways, human beings haven't changed much since those days. Then and now, the most basic reason why people love a parade is that there's a touch of the show-off in every one of us. The scientists who study human behavior say that man's desire to be noticed and admired is very nearly as important to him as his need for food, shelter, and love. This was true of the primitive caveman—thumping his chest to say "look at me!"—just as it is true of today's high-stepping, baton-twirling drum majorette. To be part of a parade is obviously an excellent opportunity for a man to strut and preen and feel that crowds of people are admiring him. Even the person too timid to do his own showing-off can stand on the sidelines and share the paraders' pride almost as much as if he were among them.

A man would feel foolish parading all by himself, but in company with a dozen or a hundred other marchers he loses his self-consciousness. This is another reason why parades have been so popular for so long—men are sociable creatures, and most of them find it easier or more pleasant to do things in a group. Somehow, when a hundred fun-loving people get together, each one of them seems to have a hundred times as much fun as he would alone. It's the same with solemn occasions—a worry, fear, or grief is easier for an individual to bear when it's shared with a multitude.

For a parade to *be* a parade, the multitude must include watchers as well as marchers. Any procession would be an absurdity if it had to march down an empty and uncaring avenue. That's why even the most serious parades include some "show-off" flourishes to attract attention. A religious procession honoring a god, saint, or some holy occasion is

THE RELIGIOUS PROCESSION. *With pomp, pageantry and billowing banners, a parade and crowds of spectators in the city of Fulda, Germany, observe the annual German Catholics' Day.*

(GERMAN INFORMATION CENTER)

usually rich in color, pomp, and spectacle—mainly, of course, to show the paraders' reverence for whatever is being celebrated, but also to impress the bystanders with that religion's grandeur and beauty. "Demonstration" marchers carry signs and banners, chant and sing. That most somber of processions, the funeral, is usually as splendid and majestic as the dead man's mourners can make it—partly out of their sincere regard for him, but partly also to invite the sympathy and respect of the onlookers. Like a stage play, a parade may be dramatic, comic, or tragic. But any parade, like any play, is a failure without an audience.

Those cavemen who started the whole idea probably never lacked for an enthusiastic audience. Indeed, their return-from-the-hunt procession must have been the only sort of public entertainment those primitive people had to brighten their harsh struggle for existence. And it would have continued to be, for a good many thousands of years, until later generations invented dancing, singing, music-making, and sports.

But the newer recreations didn't diminish the popularity of parades. By this time, men had begun to quit their hunter's life of rootless roaming in family groups and small tribes. They were becoming herders and farmers, and settling down to live in permanent communities of many people together. This community life was much more easy and comfortable. Now men had the leisure time to plan and perform all sorts of public ceremonies, both serious and for fun, on all sorts of occasions. We have evidence—in cave paintings, rock carvings, and other relics of everyday life back then—that many of those prehistoric ceremonies and celebrations either began with or included a parade of some kind.

Early men marched in procession to their "magic-making" ceremonies or to the places where they offered sacrifices to the "nature spirits." Later, when religion replaced the belief in magic and spirits, a procession was still considered a necessary part of every worship service. Any new undertaking might be launched with a parade, and the project's successful conclusion would be celebrated with one. Warriors paraded off to battle and (if they won) paraded home again. A really outstanding event, victory, or achievement might be commemorated for a long time afterward, with festivities and parades held on its anniversary year after year. Whenever a community or a nation got a new leader or ruler, the ceremony of his taking office usually included a parade. Even the milestones of ordinary family life—christenings, marriages, burials—were marked by parades, of at least the family members.

Parades are mentioned in some of the earliest writings that have been discovered. For example, archaeologists have found a scrap of ancient Egyptian writing, nearly four thousand years old, which mentions a grand procession held in honor of the god Upwawet.

Somewhat nearer our own time, about two thousand years ago, the Egyptian queen Cleopatra was fond of parades, particularly those in which she was the star. Writers from Shakespeare to modern moviemakers have inserted parades in their plays about Cleopatra, as a means of dramatizing her flamboyantly colorful personality. Shakespeare described her royal barge, in which she cruised the Nile River, as being plated with shining gold and having perfumed purple sails that gave a fragrant scent to the winds. To re-create the queen's entrance into Rome on the occasion when she visited Julius Caesar, the makers of the recent movie Cleopatra marched a most spectacular parade before their cameras.

In the ancient city of Babylon, one special avenue was laid out for no other purpose but parading. It led from the temple of the god Marduk

A GREAT PARADE OF CLASSICAL TIMES *is re-created in this spectacular scene from the motion picture* Cleopatra, *showing the Egyptian queen's triumphal entry into Rome.*

(20TH CENTURY-FOX FILM CORP.)

to the Ishtar Gate, and was wider than most city streets of today. It was walled along its length with colored tiles, adorned with statues of lions and paved with limestone blocks, every one of these bearing the carved notice: "For the procession of the great god Marduk." The parade street took more than forty years to complete and decorate in all its magnificence. Thereafter, it was the route of the city's New Year procession, when a vast image of Marduk was carried from the temple to the banks of the Euphrates River, and all of Babylon gathered for a three-day worship service.

Both Egypt and Babylon were already highly civilized nations even in those long-ago days. But in the northern wilds of Europe, too— where mankind had progressed only to the Bronze Age and was still half-savage—parades were likewise a common custom.

The barbarians of Scandinavia, for instance, worshipped the sun and believed that it made its way across the sky in some kind of invisible chariot or boat. So they imitated the sun's daily "parade" by holding parades of their own. A two thousand-year-old souvenir of one of these Bronze Age ceremonies was dug up in Denmark in recent times. It is a model of a horse and cart, carrying a gold-plated disk to represent the sun. The model was built to be the main exhibit in processions honoring the sun, when it was drawn along like a modern-day parade float.

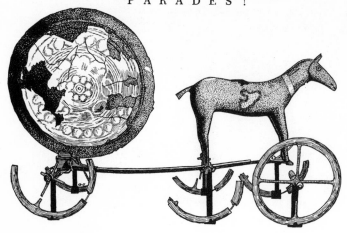

TWO THOUSAND YEARS AGO, *this wood and bronze horse and cart carried a gold-plated "sun" disk in parades honoring the sun god of the ancient Scandinavians.*

About the same time, on the other side of the world, religious parades were also customary among the prehistoric Incas of what is now the country of Peru. Their religion was partly based on reverence for their dead ancestors, and as a result their worship processions were what we would consider rather gruesome. The paraders carried litter-chairs in which rode the mummies of their dead kinsmen.

The religious parades of ancient Greece have left us one priceless piece of art. The Greek temple called the Parthenon, built some twenty-three hundred years ago on a hill above Athens, is still standing, and is famous as the most perfect piece of architecture surviving from olden times—perhaps the most perfect *ever* built. One of its features was a beautifully carved stone frieze, or border, that ran around all four sides of the temple, just below the roof cornice. (Most of this stonework is now in the British Museum.) The carved figures in this frieze represent paraders in the Panathenaic procession, which was held every year in honor of Athena, the goddess of wisdom and protector of the city.

The sculptured procession starts at the west end of the temple, with a group of young men just mounting their horses. The parade divides there, half of it marching off along each of the two side walls. It shows mounted men, horse-drawn chariots, musicians with flutes and lyres, sheep and cattle being taken along for sacrifices to Athena, men carrying olive branches (the symbol of peace) and maidens carrying baskets and trays of food offerings. Both halves of the parade come together again at the eastern front of the temple, where the procession is awaited by figures representing Athena and other goddesses and gods. Of all the pictures and depictions of parades that man has made, from Stone Age cave paintings to modern movies, the graceful Parthenon frieze is the one that most deserves to be called a work of art.

THE PARTHENON *of Athens is shown in this drawing as it looked when first built. The Panathenaic parade marches around the stone frieze between the columns and the roof.*

The ancient Romans held similar religious processions, and also circus parades of a sort, but Rome is better remembered for its military parades. The Roman army, the mightiest of its day, was forever parading off to conquer some other country or to put down a rebellion in some Roman colony. Its fighting skill and ferocity made Rome the ruler of almost all the world that was then known. So powerful and terrible were the Roman legions that sometimes they didn't even have to go into battle to win a victory. They merely had to hold a parade.

For example, if some foreign ruler resented being given orders by the Roman emperor and showed signs of refusing, he might be invited for a visit to Rome, and there he would be "entertained" with a military parade. At the sight of all those warlike legions—thousands of swordsmen, spearmen, bowmen, stone-slingers, cavalrymen, rumbling war chariots, and ponderous battering-rams—the visiting ruler would usually be so impressed and intimidated that he'd meekly agree to any demands Rome wanted to make.

The world's languages today are indebted to ancient Rome for many of their words relating to parades. The very word "parade" had its beginning in the Romans' word *parare*, Latin for "to prepare." This later became the Spanish *parada*, meaning a field where soldiers drill and train in preparation for combat. From there it was only a short step to today's "parade," signifying almost any kind of marching or moving procession, military or otherwise.

"Triumph" now means a victory. However, to the Romans, the original Latin word *triumphus* meant not the victory itself but the parade that was held to celebrate it and to welcome home its heroes. The Latin word *marcus* meant "hammer." It also came to mean the stick with which a Roman drummer thumped out the cadence for marching legionnaires. And paraders today still keep step to the *marcus*, because from that word came our "march."

In the ancient world, just as in today's, religious and military parades were ceremonies of serious intent. But some of the gayer occasions, too, had their beginnings in ceremonies that were originally solemn and even fearful. Before we go on to take a look at the parades associated with these holidays, let us see how the holidays themselves came into being.

The most important ones were those invented to honor nature—or, as the early men would have said, to honor the "nature spirits" which they believed had charge of everything in the world.

The sun was the foremost spirit. Without the sun's light and warmth nothing could live on earth. So in winter, when the sun rose later each day and set earlier, many primitive people feared that it was going away for good. As the days dwindled down to the very shortest one of the year—the winter solstice as it is called, which falls about December 21 in countries north of the equator—it became an almost worldwide custom for men to gather on that day, to hold processions, offer sacrifices, dance and chant to the sun, and plead with it to "stay." The anguished ceremony would go on and on, for a week or more, until the people became aware that the days were getting longer again—that the sun had "decided to stay"—and the gathering would turn into a jubilant celebration.

Much the same sort of thing went on at the summer solstice (about June 21 in the northern hemisphere) when the day was at its longest, when the sun had reached its topmost point of the year and was about

A DREAM PARADE, *as imagined by an artist of the Middle Ages, shows a Midsummer procession of mythological creatures, including dragons, goat-footed satyrs, and half-man-half-horse centaurs.*
(N.Y. PUBLIC LIBRARY)

to start edging down the sky again. Even long after people realized that they weren't *really* persuading the sun to do anything—that it pursued the same course year after year—the ceremonies and processions were still performed, partly out of habit, partly because the people enjoyed the get-togethers.

There were two other big celebrations each year. One was to welcome the coming of spring, when trees, flowers, and every growing thing awakened again after the long sleep of winter. Because spring comes earlier in warm climates than it does in cold, some southern communities held their celebrations as early as February, some northerners as late as May. But whenever it arrived, spring brought new life, new beginnings. Thus many nations celebrated their New Year at this time of young buds and fresh greenery—and some still do. (It was only comparatively recently that the Christian countries decided to have January 1 start the year. In Great Britain and the American colonies, New Year's Day still fell on March 25 until 1753.)

Then there was the autumn celebration, a time of mingled sadness and gladness. The year was dying, the greenery was fading into brown, and the leaves were falling. But it was also harvest time, the season of ripeness and plenty. So once more the people gathered, to give thanks to the "nature spirits" for providing good crops and fat herds, and to pray that they'd be blessed with a mild winter as well.

Of course there were many other occasions for celebration or ceremony in the ancient world—the victories, coronations, funerals, etc.— but these happened at irregular intervals and they were differently observed in different places. The four regular events of the year—

midwinter, midsummer, the coming of spring and autumn—are worth
noting because they were observed in much the same way by almost
everybody in the ancient world, and because (as we shall see) they are
still celebrated in some manner by most people in the world today.

These, mankind's oldest holidays, have changed their names and
their reasons for celebration many times over the centuries. Some of
them—and the parades that mark them—are still serious and dignified,
some are now just for fun. But as we watch the processions that march
through this book, we'll try to look beyond the banners and brass bands
for a glimpse of their histories. And we'll find that many of today's
parades have been marching since man first learned to walk.

THIS COULD EASILY *be a scene from thousands of years ago, but it's actually a
modern-day parade—the Okunchi Festival held at Karatsu, Japan, every October
to invoke a prosperous season for the local fishing fleets.*

(JAPAN NATL. TOURIST ASSN.)

II

Parades That Bloom in the Spring

EVER SINCE PREHISTORIC MAN invented the welcome-to-spring celebration, springtime has continued to be the season most thickly sprinkled with holidays and holy days.

The ancient Phoenicians held riverside ceremonies and processions in the spring of every year, to thank their goddess Astarte for bringing the springtime flood that irrigated their farmlands. In ancient Greece, the god Dionysus was believed responsible for all growing things, so the Greeks honored him with the spring festival called the *Dionysia*. Its main feature was an all-day parade that escorted a float drawn by sacred oxen, on which stood a statue of Dionysus. The parade included flute-players, trumpeters, and young men and women swinging containers of burning incense that left trails of perfumed smoke in the air. The Romans' goddess Cybele was regarded as the "mother of earth," and to her they dedicated their spring holiday called the *Hilaria* (from which comes our English word "hilarity," meaning gaiety and merriment). The Hilarian parade was much like the Greeks' Dionysian, except that Cybele's statue was drawn through the streets by a pair of tame lions. The Hindus of India have always believed that the spring is "born" of the marriage of the god Parvati and the goddess Siva. They still celebrate this yearly rebirth of the earth by holding elaborate mock-wedding processions on the spring day they call the Feast of Huli.

In Scandinavian cities during the Middle Ages it was the custom, on a springtime day, for two troops of mounted men to parade separately through the streets and out into the fields. One parade was led by a

rider dressed in heavy furs, who tossed snowballs at the spectators. The
other parade's leader wore light garments trimmed with greenery and
strewed flowers along the way. The city folk would follow the paraders
into the fields, where the two opposing troops would hold a mock-battle
with lances. The outcome of the fight was, of course, pre-arranged—as
a historian of that time remarked—"to make a publicke shew, that
Summer hath conquered Winter."

For more than six hundred years, the city of Zurich, Switzerland, has
welcomed spring with an April parade of all the local trade guilds. The
workers dress in antique costumes and carry symbols of their trade. The
barbers, for example, carry an immense pair of scissors. The hat-makers
display a giant hat. The bakers throw sweet buns to the crowd. But the
star of the parade is Boögg (pronounced "Bo-ogg"), an enormous snowman who represents Old Man Winter. At the close of the parade, Boögg
is set on a platform over a bonfire. Slowly he sags, melts, dwindles—and
then the fire reaches a container of firecrackers hidden inside him. The
resulting blast means the end of Boögg—and of winter.

One of the oldest religious festivals still observed today is the Jewish
springtime Feast of the Passover. For more than five thousand years the
Jews have celebrated this as the anniversary of the Exodus, when
Moses led their Israelite ancestors out of Egypt and out of slavery. But
scholars believe that the holiday actually dates from long before Moses'
time, and was originally the prehistoric Israelites' welcome-to-spring
ceremony.

Many Christian holidays, too, are bound up with the age-old observances of much older religions. St. Patrick's Day is one of them. Until
about fifteen hundred years ago, Ireland was one of the half-savage

A **WELCOME-TO-SPRING PARADE** *of the trade guilds in a Swiss city. These masked
marchers are recalling the legend of the Swiss hero William Tell. Notice the
bow-and-arrow-and-apple design of their headdresses.*

(SWISS NATL. TOURIST OFFICE)

BOÖGG, *the snowman representing Old Man Winter, rides in a welcome-to-spring parade in Zurich, Switzerland. At the end of the festivities he will be melted and blown apart over a giant bonfire.*

nations that worshipped all sorts of nature spirits. Then a missionary priest named Patrick came from Rome to bring the teachings of Jesus Christ, and eventually he converted all the Irish to the Christian religion. Ever since, he has been revered as the patron saint of Ireland. And, because the nature-worshipping Irish had for ages been accustomed to hold their spring celebration in mid-March, the Christian church fathers picked March 17 to be St. Patrick's Day. This enabled the Irish to keep their old-time holiday and merely change the reason for celebrating it.

In Ireland itself, St. Patrick's Day is now more of a holy day than a holiday, and is quietly observed with family get-togethers and special church services. But the Irish who emigrated to the New World found themselves among strangers with unfamiliar holidays, and so began to celebrate St. Patrick's Day more heartily, as the one day in the year when they could really proclaim their "Irishness." Now, in America, it is as riotous an occasion as the ancient Irish welcome-to-spring must have been.

The first St. Patrick's Day parade took place in New York City during the American Revolution. On March 17, 1779, four hundred Irish soldiers in the British Army, the "Volunteers of Ireland," marched from the city waterfront up Broadway to a restaurant where they enjoyed a banquet. The British Army supplied the fife-and-drum band for their parade, and also paid for their feast. This was something of a bribe to keep the Irish soldiers loyal to their English officers—because it was no secret that all Irishmen disliked being ruled by the English, and rather hoped the Americans would win the war. But the bribe didn't work. A little while after their St. Patrick's Day celebration, all four hundred of the Irish volunteers deserted from the British ranks and joined the American Army.

By the 1850's the St. Patrick's Day parade had become an annual fixture in Boston, Philadelphia, Atlanta, and many other American cities. But the parade in New York City has always been the biggest and grandest anywhere. In 1852 it stubbornly marched through a howling blizzard, though there were precious few spectators to cheer. Nowadays it is such a gala event that many a New Yorker, whatever his nationality, is pleased to wear a bit of green and become an Irishman for the day. The marchers include such unexpected organizations as the Loyal League of Yiddish Sons of Erin. Even the parade street, Fifth Avenue, used to change its white center stripe to a green one for the occasion.

The festival of St. Joseph, which is celebrated in the Spanish city of Valencia, is another survival from long before Christian times. In the far, far past, the third week in March was the occasion for everyone in that part of Spain to give his house or shop a good spring cleaning and thus make the community fit to welcome the new, bright season. Later, when the Spanish people adopted the Christian religion, the carpenters of Valencia began to make a little ceremony of sweeping out the winter's accumulation of sawdust and shavings from their shops. They burned the trash in bonfires (called *fallas*) and dedicated these to St. Joseph, the father of Jesus, who had been a carpenter himself.

Over the years, Valencia's spring cleaning ceremony grew into a whole week of festivities, parades, concerts, dances, and bullfights. And the word *fallas* became the name of gigantic figures made of wood, canvas and plaster, and standing three or four storeys tall. The figures—there may be a hundred or more of them in today's processions—may be caricatures of well-known people or depictions of events in the news. They are the work of skilled craftsmen (the descendants of those long-ago carpenters) and take months to make. For a week the *fallas* are towed along in one parade after another, and the most clever and original of them wins a prize. Then, on St. Joseph's Night (March 19), they—like their ancestral sawdust and shavings—are ceremonially burned atop high platforms at street corners and in the city plazas.

A FALLA OF VALENCIA. *Massive constructions like this one parade through the streets of the Spanish city for a week before being burned on St. Joseph's Night. This fantastic* falla *was created by the famous artist Salvador Dali (who sculptured his own portrait into it). At the left it is seen on parade. At the right it is destroyed in an eruption of flames and sparks.*

Another Christian holiday that bears the imprint of primitive customs is Easter. According to the Bible, it was in the springtime that Jesus was crucified and then rose from the dead. Christians have established the holy day of Easter in remembrance of that miracle. But the day got its popular name because, when missionaries introduced Christianity into northern Europe, they found that the natives there had long been celebrating a spring festival dedicated to their goddess Oestre. As the natives gradually adopted the Christian religion, they blended the two holy days but kept the name of the older one (Oestre became Eostra and then Easter).

A more obvious leftover from ancient times is the Easter fashion parade. This has no connection with the day's religious meaning. It derives from the old, old superstition that to wear some article of new clothing at the start of the year insures "good fortune" for the next twelve months. And, as we know, most of the world used to celebrate the New Year in this spring season.

So it has long been traditional for Easter churchgoers to wear a "new Easter outfit" and, after services, to take a stroll for the admiration of passersby. But it was only rather recently that the simple family stroll became a bustling parade—and this was another custom that had its start in New York City.

A hundred years ago, it was a treat for the working-class New Yorker, who couldn't afford much finery of his own, to make an Easter Sunday visit to Fifth Avenue and watch "the swells" on parade. These were the wealthy society folk who attended the fashionable uptown churches and then spent the afternoon strutting up and down the avenue: the men with shining top hats, gold-knobbed canes and swallowtail coats, the ladies in extravagant bonnets and hoop-skirted gowns. Fifty years later, though, the character of the parade had changed. The common people no longer stood on the sidelines and admired (or envied) the upper classes. New Yorkers were more prosperous; even the working classes could afford to dress up, and the lowliest laborer was now "as good as the best of them." So *everybody* began to parade on Easter Sunday.

Nowadays the Fifth Avenue throng gets so dense that the paraders can barely shuffle along. And, since television began to broadcast the New York parade in the 1950's, the after-church strollers have been shoved into the background by professional models hired to display new fashion designs, and by show-offs and eccentrics dressed in outrageous costumes just to get "on camera."

THIS IS A PARADE? *Well, that's what New York City calls it. This elbow-to-elbow throng on Fifth Avenue is the long-famous Easter Parade.*

(WIDE WORLD PHOTOS)

New York's may be the most famous Easter parade, but it is no longer the only one. It is imitated in many other places now, sometimes grotesquely. A certain California town, for example, sends its Easter fashion parade zipping down a mountainside, with all the paraders on *skis*.

Of all the springtime holidays the world celebrates, there is one that takes the prize for inspiring the most and biggest parades. It is observed in almost every Christian community, in some places quietly, in others with high jinks and high revelry. But especially in cities with a large Roman Catholic population—Paris, New Orleans, Rio de Janeiro, and others—the holiday just wouldn't be complete without a parade or two. Or three. Or dozens of them.

The holiday is the Carnival, and its name calls for a bit of explanation. The word comes to us from the Latin *carnelevamen,* which means "a taking-away of meat." The connection with holiday gaiety is not as farfetched as it might appear at first glance.

The forty weekdays before Easter make up the season of Lent, during which Christians are supposed to deny themselves certain pleasures —which used to be mainly the eating of meat. This they do in memory of the forty days Jesus once spent in a desert wilderness, doing without food while He prayed and meditated. Lent being a period of self-denial, the week or so just preceding it is a Christian's last opportunity (for a while) for feasting and having fun. Actually the "taking-away of meat" would more accurately describe the sober Lenten season itself, but as the word *carnelevamen* shrank into "Carnival" it came to mean the festive days just before. (The word "carnival" with a small *c* can also mean a street show, a traveling fair, or just about any sort of merry entertainment.)

Since Lent always starts on a Wednesday, the Carnival's final and most riotous day is the Tuesday just preceding, and that day is known in some languages as "Fat Tuesday." In French the expression is *mardi gras,* and you'll hear some people say "Mardi Gras" to mean not just Fat Tuesday but the entire Carnival period.

One of the world's best-known Carnival celebrations is that held in New Orleans. The Louisiana city actually starts celebrating on Twelfth Night (January 6, the twelfth night after Christmas), a good four weeks or more before Mardi Gras. Almost every evening throughout the rest of January and February is enlivened by one lavish costume ball after another. These are organized by the men's societies which the Orleanians call "krewes"—the Twelfth Night Revellers, the Elves of Oberon, the Falstaffians, etc. There are some sixty of these parties, and every city-dweller and visiting tourist yearns to be invited to one of them.

The first outdoor parade is held about ten days before Mardi Gras. The total number of parades that march during the New Orleans Carnival is hard to calculate, because even grade-school children build floats, elect a King and Queen and parade them around their schoolyards. But if you count just the big processions—those of the Krewe of Momus, the Krewe of Proteus, etc.—there are usually about a dozen, half of them held at night by torchlight. Any one of these would be a spectacular event-to-remember in any ordinary city. But in New Orleans each of them is overshadowed by the next and grander one. And *all* of these preliminary parades are rather pale and feeble compared to the Carnival's climax—the day-long parading, panoply and pandemonium of Mardi Gras itself. At midday there's the tumultuous parade along Canal Street of Rex, King of Carnival. That one has no sooner passed than it's followed by the Elks Krewe parade. At the same time, the all-Negro parade of King Zulu is marching with great clamor through another district of the city. Then, that night, there's the eye-filling torchlight parade of King Comus.

CARNIVAL NIGHT *in New Orleans in the 1890's. This parade of the Mystic Krewe of Comus was illuminated both by flaming torches and crude electric lights.*
(N.Y. PUBLIC LIBRARY)

MORE MARDI GRAS PARADERS *of the 1890's, showing the sort of grotesque costumes the Orleanians wore—and still do wear.*

The Comus parade which closes the Carnival is the oldest of New Orleans' parades, and at one time was the feature attraction. It was started in 1857, but within a few years the nighttime celebration got to be more of a street brawl than a parade. The Comus march became the revel of ruffians and rapscallions, and timid citizens stayed away from the scene.

Then, in 1872, New Orleans learned that the Carnival was to have its first royal visitor. The Grand Duke Alexis of Russia, who was then touring the United States, had heard of the famous celebration and was coming to have a look at it. The city fathers held a hasty conference; they didn't think the rowdy Comus parade was quite the thing to set before a princeling. So they quickly organized the rival parade of Rex, a more sedate affair, and displayed it to the Grand Duke during the tranquil daylight hours. Since then, although the Comus parade has long been equally respectable, the Rex parade has taken over as the biggest event of the day and the season.

The parade is preceded by policemen on motorcycles and horses; they are needed to clear a route of march through the milling crowds of spectators who jam the streets. The building fronts, store awnings, and lamp posts are hung with flags and bunting in the traditional Carnival colors: purple, blue-green, and gold. The first float is the king's, with

Rex seated high on a swaying throne, garbed in royal robes, decked in "jewels," and majestically waving a "golden" scepter. Next comes the title float with a banner announcing the parade's theme. Every year the parade is built around some unifying subject, and this is illustrated by the score or more of giant floats that follow. The theme might be "Fairy Tales," and the floats carry scenes from the stories of *Cinderella, Snow White, Sleeping Beauty,* and other classics. Or the parade may honor some great man, and the floats re-create events in his life. The characters may be represented by costumed men and women, or animated cartoon figures, or a combination of both. All of them, live and mechanical, toss souvenirs to the crowd: flowers, trinkets, balloons, and the like. The parade bands alternately play marches, jazz tunes and the Mardi Gras's official anthem, "If Ever I Cease to Love."

KING REX *on his towering golden throne leads the Mardi Gras's biggest parade along Canal Street, the main thoroughfare of New Orleans.*

(NEW ORLEANS CHAMBER OF COMMERCE)

Rex, the king, is a different man every year, some distinguished citizen chosen for his eminence in business or social affairs. His queen is a beautiful young girl from one of the city's leading families. To be chosen for this role is the highest honor a New Orleans girl can win. Of course King Comus, King Zulu, and all the other kings of the various other parades and balls have their queens, too. As a matter of fact, there is such a numerous population of Carnival queens that one New Orleans woman makes a career of running a "queen school." That is, she teaches young girls how to walk, curtsy, and move gracefully while balancing a heavy crown and wearing the heavy robes of office.

The people who watch the New Orleans parades are not just passive spectators, as they are in most cities. Almost every person on the sidelines, young and old, is dressed for the occasion. Hardly anyone is without a mask, and most of them are fully costumed, as elaborately as the parade characters. In between the scheduled parades, the spectators throng along the streets in a sort of informal parade of their own.

Unrecognizable behind their masks, the Mardi Gras celebrants feel free to cast off all restraints and shyness. They sing, dance, play pranks on one another. Strangers become instant friends. Men and women meet, embrace, kiss, and part to seek still other strangers. Elderly folk caper and cavort like children. You may meet one of the city's leading businessmen, dressed in a grass skirt and dancing the hula—or a dignified old lady striding along on stilts. The city is a bedlam of noise: music, shouts, cheers, singing, firecrackers exploding, church bells ringing, boat whistles shrilling in the harbor. This sort of thing goes on, getting more and more uproarious, until far into the night. It is not until dawn that the last, footsore, headsore celebrants totter home to bed.

A description of the New Orleans Carnival is pretty much a description of the Carnivals held everywhere else. They are all alike in being merry, noisy, colorful, full of fun—and full of parades. Only in details do they differ much from one country to another. In the mountains of Austria, for example, the Carnival celebration includes rough-and-tumble downhill races between gaily costumed skiers.

In Belgium, the Carnival parades include clowns (known there as *gilles*) who wear tall, feathered headdresses and brilliant costumes sewn all over with bells. The *gilles'* garb is actually copied from parade costumes worn by the ancient Incas of South America, and one might wonder how these found their way to the little European country of Belgium. Four centuries ago, you see, Belgium was a part of the Spanish empire—and the Carnival *gilles* adopted these costumes in honor of the Spanish conquistadors who conquered the Incas and won Peru for Spain.

THE CARNIVAL IN AUSTRIA *includes such novelties as costumed ski races through the mountains.*

(AUSTRIAN INFORMATION SERVICE)

THE CARNIVAL IN BELGIUM *stars the bell-bedecked clowns called gilles. Adults as well as the youthful paraders shown here dress up in these ancient Inca costumes.*

(BELGIAN GOVT. INFORMATION CENTER)

Parades That Bloom in the Spring

The Fat Tuesday celebration in the little town of Sigmaringen, Germany, includes a quaint local ceremony, the *Bräuteln*, or "Bride-Wooing." This dates back more than three hundred years, to 1648, when the Thirty Years' War in Europe had just ended. So many young men had gone off to that war that the maidens of Sigmaringen just couldn't find enough bachelors to marry. The mayor got the idea of paying high honor to the first man who got married, in hopes of encouraging other bachelors to come to Sigmaringen for their brides. His idea must have worked, because the ceremony has paid honor to newlywed husbands during every Carnival season since then.

Drummers, pipers, and "town heralds" in seventeenth-century knee-breeches and three-cornered hats march through the streets, trailed by crowds of the townspeople. At the door of every man who has married within the past year, or any husband celebrating his twenty-fifth or fiftieth wedding anniversary, the heralds stop and do a dance inviting him to join the parade. If he refuses he must pay a fine. If he accepts he is carried on the dancing men's shoulders through the town and to the central square, where he is cheered and applauded by the spectators. He thanks them for the honor by tossing out apples, pretzels, and sausages to the crowd.

CLOWNS, COSTUMES, CROWDS *mean Carnival anywhere, but this sprightly parade happens to be taking place in Patras, Greece.*
(ROYAL GREEK EMBASSY)

THIS BROOM BRIGADE *of "witches" participates in a German Carnival parade to sweep the streets in a symbolic "spring cleaning."*
(GERMAN INFORMATION CENTER)

THE "SCHOOL-BAG BATTALION," *dressed in beer barrels and carrot noses, prepares to march—as it has for more than one hundred years—in the Carnival parade at Haslach, Germany.*

(GERMAN INFORMATION CENTER)

HEADS UP, *these paraders in their giant papier-mâché masks march in one of the world's oldest and most famous Carnival celebrations, that held at the Riviera resort of Nice, France.*

(FRENCH EMBASSY)

In Italy the King of Carnival is not a man but a tremendous, fat giant made of straw, with his belly stuffed full of gunpowder and firecrackers. He is paraded about until midnight on Fat Tuesday (*martedì grasso* in Italian), when he is set afire. For a time he stands there, a tower of flame, and then blows apart with a drumfire of explosions.

The Italian Carnival gave us one custom that has become a part of many other parades all year round—the throwing of confetti. The custom began two hundred years ago; but, back then, what the paraders and spectators tossed at each other was fruit. A tourist visiting Italy in the eighteenth century wrote: "During the Carnival, the ladies amuse themselves in throwing oranges at their lovers; and he who has received one of these on his eye, or has a tooth beat out by it, is convinced, from that moment, that he is a high favorite with the fair one who has done him so much honor."

We can guess that people got tired of being bopped with oranges, because later they began to substitute little hard candies (which is what the Italian word *confetti* means: "sweets"). But that must have hurt when it hit, too, because the candy soon gave way to bits and streamers of colored paper, the confetti that we know today. Even that didn't please everybody. One visitor to a nineteenth-century Carnival in Paris complained that the confetti in the streets was "five inches deep the last night of the celebration. Walking was more fatiguing than in six inches of snow." And another tourist wrote home about the same time, that "you find confetti in your soup a month after a festival."

In most Christian communities, the early springtime season of parades finishes on Carnival's Fat Tuesday, and the streets are quiet until Easter Sunday brings Lent to a close. But in the city of Florence, Italy, the solemn calm of Lent ends with a bang—a real bang—in The Explosion of the Car, or *Scoppio del Carro.* According to the city's legends, this ceremony is more than nine hundred years old, and was first staged to celebrate the victorious return of the local knights from the First Crusade in the eleventh century.

On the last day of Lent—Holy Saturday, the day before Easter—a parade winds through the Florence streets. Its main feature is the *carro*, a huge, tower-like wagon drawn by a team of white oxen. The *carro* is lavishly decorated with sacred symbols and is hung all over with firecrackers. It arrives in the city square before the Cathedral of Santa Maria del Fiore just as the noon Mass in the church is coming to its end. A long wire runs from the cathedral altar up the center aisle and out the door. This is stretched tight and attached to the *carro*, from which the oxen are unhitched. As the church choir sings the "Glory to God," a priest at the altar hangs on the wire a rocket in the shape of a dove, and lights its fuse.

THE SCOPPIO DEL CARRO *in Florence, Italy. The "dove-rocket" has just hit the massive* carro—*in a moment the car's cargo of firecrackers will explode. The wire on which the dove rides from the church altar to the* carro *can be seen stretched above the crowd at the right.*

(BROWN BROTHERS)

The dove goes sparking and whizzing over the heads of the congregation, along the wire, out the door, across the square, plunges into the *carro*'s cargo of fireworks and explodes there. The tradition is that if the dove-rocket sets off an explosion of the car's firecrackers, the local farmers will enjoy a good harvest in the fall—so naturally the festival's arrangers make sure that it does. The entire wagon seems to erupt, with thunderous noise, flashing flames, and clouds of smoke, while the crowds in the square cheer and the church choir brings its hymn to a triumphant crescendo.

The *Scoppio del Carro*'s connection with farm crops suggests that it may date from even longer ago than the Crusades, that it is probably one more survival of the prehistoric spring festivals in honor of the nature spirits and all growing things. There are still more echoes of the ancient welcome-to-spring in some other holidays observed around this time of year.

The first day of May used to be festively celebrated all through northern Europe. Early on May Day morning, all the people of a community would march in procession into the nearest woods. In some places, each of the marchers dressed in a costume decorated according to his or her occupation. English milkmaids, for instance, who were accustomed to carry milk pails on their heads every other day of the year, on this day wore massive headdresses made of pewter vases, kitchenware, plates, and silver cutlery.

There is a legend that a May Day parade in Padstow, England, once saved the country from an enemy invasion. During the Seven Years' War between England and France, says the story, a French fleet sneaked into Padstow Bay and put ashore a raiding party. But the invaders caught a glimpse of May Day paraders, all in scarlet and green costumes, the milkmaids glittering with tableware. The Frenchmen mistook them for a marching troop of well-armed English soldiers. They scrambled back to their ships and hastily sailed away.

Arriving at the forest, the May Day paraders would select a tall, straight tree, cut it down and strip it of all but its topmost greenery. A team of oxen dragged this back to town, where the people decorated it with flowers, ribbons, and flags. Now it was stood up again as the Maypole, intended to be a symbol of fruitfulness and growth. Young men and maidens danced about it, the prettiest girl was crowned Queen of the May, and the entire community spent the day in feasting and games.

A different sort of Maytime parade had its beginnings in ancient Rome. The Romans called it the *Ambarvalia,* a religious ceremony intended to protect their budding crops from storm and disease during the rest of the growing season. A procession of people, chanting and waving olive branches, would march around the edge of each planted field, driving before them a bull, a sheep, and a pig. When they had completed the circuit of all their fields, they would slaughter the three animals as a sacrifice to Ceres, the goddess of agriculture.

This ritual was continued in parts of Britain, France, and Germany, with the name of Beating the Bounds or The Boundary Walk. By the Middle Ages, the animal-sacrifice part of the ceremony had been discontinued, and the parade itself was done for a quite practical purpose. In those times, there was no such thing as surveying, so the parade became a means of refreshing the people's memory as to where each family's and each township's land began and ended. Every May, all the members of a community would troop around and inspect all the local boundary markers and fences. Sometimes the expression "beating the bounds" really fit the occasion, because, in some localities, at each boundary stone all the youngsters in the parade were given a hearty beating, on the theory that it would make them remember the markers better. In the few places where The Boundary Walk is still practiced nowadays, it is no more than an excuse for a neighborly get-together.

III

From High Summer to Deep Winter

AFTER THE WELCOME-TO-SPRING, the next biggest holiday in mankind's calendar has always been Midsummer Day. In Europe, from the beginning of history to the coming of Christianity, this longest day of the year was celebrated with bonfires on mountain peaks. People used to jump through the flames "for luck." If a pair of lovers jumped over the fire hand-in-hand they would "never be parted." In the islands of Greece it was the custom, as recently as forty or fifty years ago, for a person to leap through the flames with a stone on his head, exclaiming, "I jump over the hare's fire. A stone is on my head." Nobody seems to know *what* this was supposed to mean.

The Germans celebrated Midsummer Day with a sort of "march of the sun." Huge wooden wheels, standing seven feet high and weighing as much as eight hundred pounds, were trundled to the tops of hills and wrapped in straw. After sundown the wheels were set afire and let loose to thunder blazing down the dark hillsides. This was meant to demonstrate that the sun would be "going downhill" for the next six months. The custom came to have other meanings, too. In some places, if the wheel stayed alight all the way to the bottom of the hill, the people in the neighborhood expected to have good luck for the rest of the year. Elsewhere it was believed that the farmer on whose land the wheel finally stopped its "parade" would have the best harvest in the area.

When Europe embraced the Christian religion, the people didn't give up their various Midsummer Day traditions; they merely transferred them to the various Christian holy days that fall about the same time —St. John's Day, St. Paulinus's Day, Corpus Christi, and others.

A MIDSUMMER CELEBRATION, *this one in medieval France, shows wooden-shoed peasants taking turns leaping through the traditional bonfire "for luck."*

Bonfires are still lighted here and there in Europe during the night of June 23, the eve of St. John's Day. In France, youngsters of farm communities take turns jumping over the flames, in the belief that the local grain will grow as high as the highest jump. In some districts of France, shepherds parade their sheep with wreaths of flowers on their heads, then later nail the wreaths to their stable doors to "protect" the animals from injury or illness.

St. John shares June 24 with St. Paulinus, to whom the Roman Catholic Church also dedicates that day, and in the town of Nola, Italy, it's the time for The Lilies of Nola to parade in the saint's honor. These lilies are surely the biggest "flowers" ever seen. They are really wooden towers, eighty or ninety feet high. Each trade guild in the town—the association of tailors, that of the carpenters, etc.—builds one of these lilies and adorns it all over with terraces, turrets, holy statues, and carvings, hoping to outdo every other guild's lily in beauty and splendor. On the first level of each tower stands a *fanfara*, or band of trum-

ST. JOHN'S DAY *in the town of Braga, Portugal, is the occasion for a Mid-summer parade of maskers and giants.*

(CASA DE PORTUGAL)

peters. On the several upper levels perch children in the costumes of cherubs, angels, and saints. And on the highest level of all, under a flowered arch, stands the loveliest young lady the guild can find. By parade time, each of these towers—completely decorated and full of people—weighs two tons or more. But it is somehow hoisted onto the shoulders of forty stout men. Then, to the music of the trumpeters inside it, this gigantic tower *dances* around the Square of St. Paulinus —swaying and teetering dizzily, but never falling or shaking loose its human cargo.

The ancient Midsummer celebrations always featured heaps and masses of flowers—worn in people's hair or hung about their necks, woven into bowers and arbors, strung in garlands and wreaths—and we find flowers still abundant in the various Corpus Christi observances in Roman Catholic countries. The feast of Corpus Christi (meaning "Christ's Body") pays honor to the holy bread and wine used in the Catholic Communion service. It is a moveable feast, sometimes falling in late May but usually celebrated about mid-June.

It always includes a stately religious parade, bearing crosses, holy objects, and images of saints. But in several towns of Spain and Italy,

the beauty is not so much *in* the parade as *under* it. The townspeople
work for a whole day beforehand to carpet all the streets of the parade
route with fresh flowers, and each householder tries to make his section
of the street the loveliest of all. They chalk out designs on the pavement
—geometrical figures, Biblical scenes, angels, heraldic coats-of-arms—
and then fill in the outlines with the petals of roses, carnations, sunflow-
ers, violets, every flower that's in bloom at the time. No one is allowed
to walk on the streets before parade time, and the flower decorations
are repeatedly sprinkled to keep them fresh. The procession takes place
in the evening. Though the marchers' feet soon trample out the colorful
pictures, the crushed petals add an extra dimension of enjoyment to the
parade—a heavenly fragrance filling the air.

CORPUS CHRISTI, *another Midsummer festival, is celebrated with a flowery, water-
borne parade on Austria's Traun Lake.*
(AUSTRIAN INFORMATION SERVICE)

A STREET OF FLOWERS *is laid down in Gen-
zano, Italy, as the route of the Corpus
Christi parade. Many other towns in Italy,
Spain, and Portugal make similarly dazzling
designs of fresh flower blossoms along their
parade streets on this occasion.*
(ITALIAN STATE TOURIST OFFICE)

A one-time Corpus Christi celebration in the town of Coventry, England, gave the world one of its most famous and unusual parades. Coventry started celebrating Corpus Christi back in the thirteenth century, when England belonged to the Roman church, and the day's parade was led by a man and woman marching naked—or very nearly so—to impersonate Adam and Eve. When the Puritans came to power in 1649, under Oliver Cromwell, they sternly put an end to the parade. (The Puritans disapproved of people having fun, almost as much as they disapproved of nudity.) About thirty years later, after the Puritan government had fallen, the town reinstated the celebration as Coventry Fair. But now, instead of Adam and Eve, the parade was led by a naked lady out of an old legend.

In the eleventh century, Coventry and the country thereabout were ruled by Leofric, Earl of Mercia, a cruel tyrant. His gentle wife Godiva felt sorry for their people and begged her husband to be kinder to them. He said he would, on one condition—if she would ride through the marketplace of Coventry clad in nothing but her long hair. Lord Leofric fully expected that she'd never do such a thing, but she did. Or so says the story.

The people were so grateful for Lady Godiva's gesture on their behalf that they stayed indoors on the day she made her ride through town, and no one looked out to embarrass her. No one, that is, but one—a tailor named Thomas, who slyly peeked from his window to watch her ride by. According to the story, God struck him blind for his impudence. (Actually, the Godiva legend was centuries old before some storyteller added Thomas to it, but he put the term "Peeping Tom" into our language.)

The legend of the ride is *only* a legend, but there really was a Lady Godiva, and Coventry commemorated her as the star of the summer fair which drew visitors from all over Britain. Every year some local girl volunteered to ride a white horse in the parade, wearing her hair (or a long wig) loose about her. Probably she never rode entirely nude, but donned close-fitting, flesh-colored tights. Anyway, she hasn't ridden since the 1870's. Although the Coventry Fair is still held, the city has become too dignified and modest to parade any more Lady Godivas.

Except for its unique star attraction, the Coventry Fair was much like other Midsummer festivities held in England in earlier times. For example, there was The Riding of the George, which paraded through the town of Norwich every year on a Tuesday in late June. This had originally been a celebration of "summer's conquering winter," but the Christian elders changed it into a celebration of "St. George's conquering the dragon" (although St. George's own feast day comes two months earlier, on April 23).

LADY GODIVA'S PARADE *through the marketplace of Coventry, England. Lady Godiva never really made that famous ride, but this is artist John Collier's idea of how she'd have looked, if she had.*

St. George is the patron saint of England, and the Norwich parade acted out the most famous event in his legendary career, his slaying of a loathsome dragon that was about to dine on a young princess. The procession was led by a man in armor on a white horse, who jabbed with his lance at a mock-monster made up of one man carrying a huge, fierce dragon-head and several other men galumphing along behind under a cloth body. Although St. George was the hero of the parade, the "villain" soon became the most popular character in it. He was given the name of Snap the Dragon, and everybody loved him. He would trade jokes with spectators in the crowd, roll over and do other tricks, roguishly snap his jaws at pretty girls and giggling children.

The way was cleared for him through the crowd by four "whifflers," expert jugglers in clownish costumes who performed rather like today's baton twirlers, except that they used sharp swords. The whifflers flung the gleaming blades spinning high in the air, and never failed to catch them by their hilts. Many years after The Riding of the George had ceased to be held, people forgot what whifflers were, and some scholars

were puzzled by the word in Shakespeare's play, *King Henry V*, where
the Prologue says:

> " . . . the deep-mouth'd sea,
> Which like a mighty whiffler 'fore the King
> Seems to prepare his way . . ."

The parade also included two immense human figures, images twenty
feet tall carried by a man inside each. They represented two legendary
giants, Gog and Magog, who supposedly lived in England in ancient
days. Then there was Hob-Nob, the first "hobby horse," a man wearing
a horse costume about his waist so that he appeared to be riding it.
There were Florizel and Perdita (traditional names for a shepherd and
shepherdess). There were the Dick-Fools and Jack-Puddings, jesters
dressed in motley colors, who capered along jingling bells and playing
pranks on the spectators. In one parade, a Jack-Pudding carried a dog
under his arm like a bagpipe, with the dog's tail in his mouth like the
pipes' blowing tube, and bit the tail at intervals to make the dog squall
and the spectators laugh. People were not very tenderhearted in those
days.

There was the character called Wodewose, the Man of the Woods.
An obvious leftover from the prehistoric nature-worship ceremonies, he
was dressed all in green leaves and flowers from head to toe, and
danced along playfully squirting water on the bystanders. He was accompanied by a beautiful maiden who had been elected that year's
queen of the festival, or Midsummer Bride. In later years, Wodewose
and his bride gradually changed into Robin Hood (another man of the
woods, likewise garbed in green) and his Maid Marian.

DICK-FOOLS AND JACK-PUD-
DINGS, *making merry as they
march through an English
village in an old-time Midsummer parade.*
(N.Y. PUBLIC LIBRARY)

Another summertime parade—this one halfway around the world from England—has put another word into the English language. Every year, in June or July, Hindus from all over India visit the town of Puri for a festival, the Rath Jatra, in honor of their god Jagannath (meaning "lord of the world"). The high point of this holy day is a parade during which the people drag the immense "car of Jagannath" from the Puri temple to a building called the Gondicha Nour ("gods' house") a mile and a half away.

The car of Jagannath is forty-five feet high (as tall as a three-storey house), thirty-five feet square at the base, and has three sixteen-foot-high wheels on each side. On top of it is an idol head of Jagannath, painted white, with a hideously ugly face and stubby arms projecting from where the ears should be. Every seventeen years, this idol is replaced with a new one, and tradition demands that each new image be carved from the wood of a *nim* tree on which no crow has ever perched. Inside the idol is a small box containing a blob of quicksilver, which is supposed to represent Jagannath's soul.

At parade time, as many as four thousand worshippers seize the many long ropes attached to this ponderous vehicle. Chanting over and over, "Victory to Jagannath!" they tow it along the road, accompanied by the bang and blare of *ghunt* and *cooree* (brass gong and trumpet). Behind the lurching, creaking, groaning car of Jagannath come the similar but slightly smaller cars of his brother-god Bulbhudra and sister-goddess Subhudra. So heavy are these three machines that, even with thousands of people straining on the ropes, the mile-and-a-half journey takes several hours.

"LORD OF THE WORLD" JAGANNATH (*on the left*), *with his sister and brother in the Puri, India, temple. At the Rath Jatra festival, the three idols parade in the immense machines that inspired the dread word "juggernaut."*
(N.Y. PUBLIC LIBRARY)

In times past, it is said, the worshippers would get so carried away by the excitement and religious fervor of the occasion that they would throw themselves under the car's massive wheels—hundreds of them at every festival—giving their lives as sacrifices to Jagannath. This is probably an exaggerated story, but it's quite likely that people did slip under the wheels accidentally from time to time. Anyway, the legend that the car rolled mercilessly over these people has put Jagannath's name into our language—now slightly changed to the word "juggernaut"—to mean a monster machine, human tyrant, or any terrible force that crushes or defeats anything that gets in its way.

Now the world rounds the final corner of the year, into autumn. This season's fading greenery and shortening days have long made many people think of death—and decide that this is the time to pay honor to their dead relatives and friends.

In ancient Britain, centuries before the Christian era, October 31 was the day on which people marched in procession to the graveyards and held services for the departed. It was believed that otherwise the dead might rise up from their graves in anger and do all kinds of mischief to the living. Later, the Christian church gave October 31 the name of All Hallows' Eve; that is, the night before the day which honors all the hallowed (holy) saints of the church. But the people of Britain continued to associate that date with the dead, with ghosts, witches, and other evil spirits. It still has those associations, though they're now taken lightly and humorously, as our Halloween.

In the British Isles and America, we no longer march to the graveyards, but the day still has its parades. Children throng the cities' streets in costume, carrying lighted jack-o'-lanterns and imitating "evil spirits" by ringing doorbells, soaping store windows and the like. However, their custom of trooping from door to door and demanding "trick or treat!" is much newer than the other traditions of Halloween. It dates only from the seventeenth century, when, in Ireland, poor people used to knock at the doors of their richer neighbors on All Hallows' Eve, to beg money with which to buy the makings of a feast for the morrow's holy day.

In other parts of Europe, it was two days later, on November 2, that people made their processions to the graveyards. The Roman Catholic Church gave the occasion the name of All Souls' Day, but in most languages it is still called simply The Day of the Dead (*Jour de Morts* in French, *Giorno dei Morti* in Italian, etc.), and the people still parade to the cemeteries, all in mourning clothes and led by the local priests. There they tidy up the gravesites and decorate them with flowers and candles. In olden times they would leave offerings of food and drink for the graves' occupants. Nowadays they oftener hold a picnic for the living.

Until quite recent times, the Chinese observed a similar autumn occasion, The Feast of the Hungry Souls, at which time they believed the spirits of the dead returned to earth for a "holiday." To provide these spirits with all the necessary conveniences, the Chinese made paper models of houses, furniture, clothing, even automobiles. They also printed paper money for the spirits to spend, some of it inscribed "Issued by the Underworld Bank." All of these things were burned, to "release their spirits" for the use of the dead souls. Then the Chinese went to the nearest riverbank, for one of the oddest and prettiest parades ever staged—a parade of paper boats.

Each family brought to the river a paper boat with a candle set in it—the intention being to "light the way back to earth" for the returning dead. Some of the boats were the simple folded things that children still make, but some of them were big and elaborate, wearing full sets of paper sails and complete with paper crew and passengers—including a paper King of Hell and his demon assistants. After dark, the candle-bearing boats were floated all at once, in a flotilla that might extend from one bank of the river to the other. Slowly they drifted out of sight until they were visible only as a fleet of twinkling lights. Gradually the boats became waterlogged and sank, and the tiny flames winked out one by one, until all were gone on their journey to the "other world."

But other, less solemn festivals have always been held about this same time of year, because it is also the season for bringing the harvest home. In ancient days, the Jews used to move from their homes to temporary camps in the fields while they reaped their crops, and there they would celebrate the open-air Feast of the Ingathering. The ancient Romans held parades around their fields, and a feast to give thanks to Pomona, their goddess of orchards. In medieval Britain, the season was known as Gossomer ("Goose Summer"), the time to eat the goose that had been fattening all summer long.

In Europe, now, the harvest festival is generally celebrated on St. Martin's Day (November 11). The traditional dinner of the day in most countries is still roast goose, and in Sweden the occasion is actually called Marten Gås, or "Martin's Goose" day. In the United States we have an identical celebration on Thanksgiving Day, the last Thursday in November. The American holiday dates from 1621, when the Pilgrims of the Plymouth Colony gathered to give thanks for their first harvest—and our traditional Thanksgiving dinner is roast turkey because that was what the Pilgrims ate at their feast.

In many places, both in America and Europe, parades are held on

THE AUTUMN'S HARVEST-HOME *celebration is observed in a Flanders town with a parade that includes all the local flocks and herds.*

this harvest-home day. For example, in Germany and the Netherlands, it is on St. Martin's Day (instead of Halloween) that the children parade with jack-o'-lanterns made of scooped-out pumpkins, turnips, and beets. But nowhere in the world is there such a spectacular Thanksgiving parade as that staged in New York City. Admittedly, it has little to do with giving thanks; its prime purpose is to persuade New Yorkers that now is the time to start their Christmas shopping. But the parade's purely profit motive doesn't make it any less enjoyable to watch.

It is sponsored by Macy's department store, and has been held every Thanksgiving since 1924. That year, about ten thousand people turned out to see it. Nowadays it is seen by more people than have ever watched any other procession (excepting only the funerals of President Kennedy and Sir Winston Churchill). About 2 million New Yorkers crowd along Central Park West and Broadway to watch it pass, and television carries it to 67 million more spectators across the continent.

The parade includes magnificent floats, Santa Claus in his sleigh, high school bands from all over the country, stars of the movies, television, and the sports world, and some two thousand costumed marchers —most of them employees of the Macy's store (including the store's top executives, who particularly like to enact the clowns).

But the parade's most distinctive feature is its giant balloons—Bullwinkle Moose, Linus the Lion, Elsie the Cow, the Underdog, Donald Duck, and more. These balloons are almost as big as blimps—the tail-wagging Dino the Dinosaur is seventy feet long—and they overtop many of the high New York buildings the parade passes. Each balloon takes three to four months to construct, about fifty gallons of paint to decorate, and seven or eight hours to be pumped full of helium on Thanksgiving morning. Once filled with the lighter-than-air gas, each balloon requires as many as forty men to hold it down during the parade. On one occasion, one of the balloons soared away and an airplane nearly ran into it. Another time, one of them broke loose and drifted out to sea. Until it finally vanished somewhere in mid-Atlantic, the Coast Guard kept getting radio reports from ships that strange monsters were rising out of the depths.

The remaining great festival of the ancient world's calendar—the Midwinter Day celebration—is still with us, its traditions and ceremonies now divided between our Christmas and New Year observances. For example, our custom of exchanging gifts at Christmas came from ancient Rome's midwinter festival called the *Saturnalia*, when the Romans gave presents to each other and even to their slaves. The Christmas tree and the hanging mistletoe are part of our holiday tradition because the evergreen tree and the white-berried plant were worshipped by the people of northern Europe long before Christian times.

OVERHEAD, THE "UNDERDOG," *a television cartoon character—now magnified to the size of a blimp—is one of the balloons that soar above New York's world-famous Thanksgiving Day parade.*

CHRISTMAS DAY, *in Old New York, was an occasion for rowdy parades. This is an artist's interpretation of one that marched—or surged—up Broadway in the 1880's.*

In many places, Christmas Eve is the occasion for elaborate religious processions, and in the cities of England and America bands of "waits," or carol singers, troop from house to house serenading the occupants with Christmas hymns and carols. In parts of Wales, England, and Germany, the even older custom called Hodening is still practiced. This is a parade of children, one or more of them astride a broomstick horse whose head is sometimes a real horse's skull with a candle inside, and sometimes made of wood with a jaw that champs ferociously at the pull of a string. The Hodening paraders march from door to door, as children do on Halloween in other places, to "frighten" the householders into giving them a treat or risking a trick.

But, because Christmas is a solemn religious holiday, most of the rowdier parades handed down from the old Midwinter Day celebrations have been kept for New Year's Day. In Sweden, for instance, January 1 has long been a day for merrymaking, and Swedish immigrants to the New World brought the custom with them when they settled in Pennsylvania in colonial times. On New Year's Day they would put on masks and costumes and parade through the countryside.

Their British-born neighbors joined in the fun and imitated their own traditional "mummers" (the traveling players of old England) by acting out the legend of St. George versus the dragon. After the Revolution, St. George was replaced by George Washington as the hero of these parades.

The Mummers' Parade still marches through Philadelphia every New Year's Day. Various men's clubs and business associations compete to put on the best show. (They change their clubs' names for the occasion to titles like The Early Risers, The Mixed Pickles, and The Energetic Hoboes). The parade is divided into two separate sections. The comic division acts out comedy versions of current events and makes fun of various local politicians and celebrities. Meanwhile, the marchers in the fancy-dress division compete for the money prizes awarded for the best costumes. In some years, the prizes, donated by the city government and the clubs sponsoring the parade, have totaled as much as $30,000. The parade is composed of some twelve thousand marchers, all of them men. If any female characters are required in the comedy skits, they are impersonated by men. The music for the parade is traditionally provided by bands of banjo players, but the more familiar brass bands also take part.

Not as old as the Philadelphia Mummers' Parade, but even more famous, is the Tournament of Roses held in Pasadena, California, every New Year's Day. On that day in 1886, the members of a Pasadena club loaded their horse-drawn carriages and buggies with bunches of roses, and drove around the town. This little outing was intended to celebrate the ripening of the local orange crop (an event which supposedly occurs each year about January 1). Within a few more years, the parade included flower-decorated motor cars, and then floats especially built for the occasion. The parade has continued to expand in size and showiness until now it is one of America's gaudiest street shows.

It grew so much, indeed, that the Pasadena authorities had to set a limit on it. Now the parade can include no more than sixty floats, and only ten of these may advertise a commercial firm or product. The remainder are sponsored by civic, religious, military, and fraternal organizations of the United States, Canada, and Mexico. The parade also includes some twenty bands—about 2,000 musicians altogether—and about 150 mounted police, "cowboys," and "desert sheiks" riding silver-saddled Thoroughbred, Arabian, and palomino horses.

Each year's Tournament has a different theme—patriotic, historical, or whatever (the 1966 theme was "It's a Small World")—and the theme has to be announced in the preceding April, because most of the floats are so fantastically huge and elaborate that they take many months to design and build. Usually a float begins with a steel-bar framework laid upon a truck chassis, and is built up to final form with plywood, shaped chicken-wire and sprayed-on plastic.

The float's final decoration, though, is not done until New Year's morning, just before the parade begins—because it requires thousands of flower blooms that must be dewy fresh. Often these have to be flown into Pasadena that very morning, from as far away as Hawaii. The early Tournaments relied mainly on roses, which are grown locally, but now the floats are covered with all colors of camellias, carnations, chrysanthemums, rare tropical orchids, and just about every other kind of flower you can name. Each float requires about thirty people to do the rush job of pinning on the flower blooms just before parade time.

THE TOURNAMENT OF ROSES, *held every New Year's Day in Pasadena, California, is famous for its colossal floats, each one decorated and colored with thousands upon thousands of fresh, fragrant flower blossoms.*

(PASADENA TOURNAMENT OF ROSES. J. ALLEN HAWKINS)

At one New Year's or another, the floats have carried such center-pieces as an airplane, a San Francisco cable car, a dinosaur, a whale, soaring staircases and balconies, a Noah's Ark, statues of baseball heroes, a Mississippi River showboat—all of these either life-size or super-giant-size, and all completely covered and colored with fresh, fragrant flower blossoms. Some floats have carried such other decorations as splashing waterfalls, live birds and animals, and fountains spraying perfume.

Each float has its pretty, smiling Queen aboard, and the parade as a whole has its supreme Queen of the Tournament of Roses, who rides a float of her own. She and her six attendant Princesses are elected each year from among the girl students of Pasadena City College. The parade is led by a celebrity invited to be Grand Marshal, and in years past these marshals have included such notables as movie stars Mary Pickford, Shirley Temple, Bob Hope, and ex-Presidents Herbert Hoover and Dwight Eisenhower.

Two other cities in California enjoy another New Year's celebration a month or so later. This festival, the Chinese New Year, can be seen in several other American cities—New York, Honolulu, etc.—but the best place to view it is either San Francisco or Los Angeles. The "Chinatown" districts of these two cities are the largest Chinese communities anywhere outside China itself, and their celebrations of the holiday are probably gayer and livelier than the festivities *inside* China.

THE CHINESE NEW YEAR *comes in with a roar, as the traditional parade dragon coils and curvets through the narrow streets of San Francisco's Chinatown.*
(SAN FRANCISCO CHRONICLE)

According to the ancient Chinese calendar, New Year's Day—or the first day of the first moon—may fall anywhere between January 21 and February 19. In olden times, the holiday lasted for a solid month thereafter, and, to buy the necessary decorations, food, liquor, and entertainment, a Chinese family would often be obliged to spend every penny it had saved during the whole preceding year. In more recent times, the holiday was shortened to just two weeks (and in America to one week). Most of the celebrating during this period is done within the family circle, but the festivities spill out into public view now and again, with someone setting off a string of firecrackers, or a band of musicians banging and tweedling through the streets. And the holiday traditionally concludes with a big, noisy, colorful nighttime parade, attended by the entire community.

Officially the parade is The Festival of Lanterns. In old China, this was the occasion for everyone to try to outdo everybody else in fashioning the most beautiful and most original sort of lantern to carry in the procession. Most of them were made of translucent colored paper, in the shapes of balls, cubes, pagodas, fans, sheep—and later even automobiles, trolley cars, airplanes, and refrigerators. But by far the most striking were the lanterns carved from ice and lighted by oil lamps inside. Some of these ice lanterns were in the shape of life-sized human beings.

The lanterns are less important, now, and serve only to light the way for the star of the parade—the famous Chinese dragon. Made of cloth stiffened with bamboo rods, this merry monster is sometimes a hundred feet long and requires as many as fifty men inside to make it march, dance, waggle, and lunge threateningly at the spectators. Its wooden or plaster head has glaring gold-and-blue eyes, silver horns dangling red silk tassels, a long green beard, and a gaping mouth from which lolls a red velvet tongue. Sometimes the long body is lighted by hundreds of candles stuck along its sides.

If a modern New Year's parade follows its traditional form, there'll be one man capering along the street ahead of the dragon and teasing it with a large ball made of many-colored ribbons. The dragon chases and snaps at the ball, but it is always snatched away from him. In China, the parade watchers used to help confuse the dragon by shooting at him with small hand-cannons—bamboo tubes charged with gunpowder and iron filings. This aspect of the parade is evidently left over from some long-ago ceremony marking the shortest day of midwinter. The dragon seems to represent the winter, and the ball to symbolize the returning sun "escaping" from winter's grasp.

Nowadays, in the Chinatowns of America, the dragon usually snaps at money instead. At each shop the parade passes, the merchants hold out a bit of money, enclosed in a red paper envelope, tucked inside a tangerine, or rolled into a lettuce leaf—and the passing dragon gulps and "swallows" it. The money is a donation to the Chinatown association that puts on the parade.

Other features of the New Year's parade, once traditional, are missing now. In the villages of old China, the marchers included men costumed as the Fisherman, the Old Woman, the Woodcutter, and other typical village personalities—all of them teetering along on high stilts. In some places, a group of men danced while carrying a tremendously tall pole, on the very top of which a fearless little girl somehow managed to stand and keep her balance.

Then there was the "Dry Boat," in which a beautiful maiden was rowed along the street by her sweetheart. In truth, both the girl and the rower were men, wearing a boat-shaped construction around their waists. The boat was made of bent willow branches and covered with a cloth that hung down to the ground to conceal their legs. One of the men heaved on a pair of oars. The other was painted and costumed to resemble a girl, and wore an extra pair of "legs" which were gracefully arranged on top of the boat. It all sounds quite ridiculous, but people who've seen it say that the illusion was remarkably realistic. As the men walked along in a sort of swooping glide, you could almost believe you were watching a pair of lovers in a real boat, really drifting along a real river.

ANOTHER VIEW *of the San Francisco Chinatown parade. These 15-foot-tall giants, glistening with bright paints and costumes, were specially ordered from Hong Kong just for the city's New Year observance.*
(S. F. CONVENTION & VISITORS BUREAU)

IV

The One-of-a-Kind Parades

So far, we have been viewing mainly the parades which celebrate seasonal or religious occasions. Since they are common to large numbers of the world's people, they are usually observed in many places at about the same time and in about the same way. But there are numerous days in the year that are "special" to only one country, or to one community, or even to one small group of people within that community—and the parades held on these days often have no counterparts anywhere else on earth.

Just about every nation holds festivities and parades to mark the anniversary of its discovery, founding, or independence; to honor its national heroes; to commemorate the wars it has won; to boast of whatever resources, qualities, or advantages it has that other countries haven't. And naturally these reasons vary from one nation to the next.

In most of the United States, we celebrate the discovery of the New World on Columbus Day, October 12. The first time the day got any attention was in 1792, the three-hundredth anniversary of Columbus's voyage, when a New York men's society held a small parade, gave a dinner and erected a miniature monument to the explorer in their club headquarters. During the next century, if the day was observed at all, it got no great notice—until October 12, 1892, the four-hundredth anniversary of America's discovery.

Then New York City threw the biggest Columbus Day parade held to this day, and one of the longest parades of any sort *ever* held. When it stepped off along Fifth Avenue at ten o'clock that Wednesday morning, it was not outstandingly spectacular in its makeup. It consisted merely of the usual brass bands, tableau floats, and ranks of marching men—but so many of each that the parade didn't finish until 2 a.m. on Thursday. During all those sixteen hours, people were packed so tightly along the avenue that the parade had to include ambulances at intervals between the marching units, to pick up the spectators who fainted from the crush.

We may not see anything like that again (or want to) until the *five*-hundredth anniversary in 1992. But the Columbus Day parade has been an annual event in many big cities ever since that time in 1892. For one reason, that was the era when Italians were emigrating to the United States in great numbers. And, just as the Irish-Americans had made St. Patrick's Day "their" holiday, the Italo-Americans seized on Columbus Day as the opportunity to demonstrate *their* pride in their ancestry. So the parade's marchers still consist mainly of people of Italian descent.

By now, practically every national group in America has a "folk holiday" of its own. The Polish-Americans proudly parade on October 11, the anniversary of the death of Count Casimir Pulaski, a Polish nobleman who helped fight the British during the American Revolution. Americans of Scandinavian descent parade on October 9, Leif Ericsson Day, to honor the Viking who evidently discovered America long before Columbus did.

A WILD WEST PARADE? *No, it's a pistol-packing platoon of riders in the town of Kalamai, Greece, celebrating the nation's Independence Day.*
(ROYAL GREEK EMBASSY)

Of all our cities, probably only New York gets to see *all* these various "folk parades"—and many others besides: Greek, Puerto Rican, Negro, Croatian, and so on—because its population includes just about every nationality there is. Other cities have to make do with just the parades of whatever foreign nationalities are most numerous among their citizens. Of course, every city in the nation has the opportunity to stage a parade on the several patriotic, all-American holidays such as Independence Day (July 4), Flag Day (June 14), and Citizenship Day (September 17).

However, the entire nation doesn't always agree as to which of these holidays call for a parade. Even Columbus Day is observed in only forty of the fifty states. And many localities have their own one-of-a-kind patriotic holidays. On March 2, the state of Texas celebrates the day (in 1836) on which it declared its independence from Mexico and became, briefly, the Republic of Texas. Although Hawaii is now one of the United States, its biggest holiday is Kamehameha Day (June 11), honoring the nineteenth-century King Kamehameha I, who first united the separate islands into the Kingdom of Hawaii. In Maine and Massachusetts, even Independence Day rates only the "second best" parades, in comparison to the grand processions that march on Patriots' Day (April 19).

KAMEHAMEHA DAY, *Hawaii's biggest holiday, is observed with a parade that includes these lovely* pa-u *lady riders, decked in flowing gowns and leis of flowers.*

(HAWAII VISITORS BUREAU)

A person could get quite a good education in American history just by wandering around the country and watching the parades on these various holidays. The typical Columbus Day parade includes a tableau float showing the admiral planting the flag of Spain in this new hemisphere. Cape Henry Day in Virginia (usually April 26) and Forefathers' Day in the New England states (December 21) both commemorate the arrival of the first groups of English colonists who settled on this continent. And practically every state has a holiday—Pennsylvania Day, Indiana Day, Arizona Admission Day, and so on—to celebrate either its founding or its entrance into the Union.

Such local observances as the Battle of Bennington Day in Vermont (August 16) and Bunker Hill Day in Boston, Massachusetts (June 17) provide a blow-by-blow account of the Revolution. The War of 1812 is recalled in such holidays as Andrew Jackson Day in Louisiana (January 8, anniversary of his victory in the Battle of New Orleans) and Defenders' Day in Maryland (September 12, anniversary of the Battle of North Point). The parades on Memorial Day (May 30 in most states) honor the dead of the Civil War. Veterans Day (November 11, formerly called Armistice Day) pays tribute to the American soldiers who fought in World Wars I and II and the Korean War.

This list of parade days could go on and on, and we could fill in many more details of America's history by including such celebrations as the Frontier Days of Cheyenne, Wyoming. This festival week every July re-creates the scenes, costumes, customs, and sports of Cheyenne's "cowboy era" (and all the men taking part in the festivities and parades have to grow Old West-style beards and mustaches for the occasion). Probably you can think of other parade days to add to the "American history" list. Perhaps your own community celebrates some hometown hero or noteworthy event in its past.

CALGARY, ONTARIO, *re-lives its frontier days with the annual celebration called the Calgary Stampede. Here, in the festival's big street parade, local Indians ride on horses dragging* travois *pack-poles.*

(CALGARY EXHIBITION & STAMPEDE)

Then there are the parade days that teach geography. Many an American city or county takes pride in some local feature and builds a festival or a parade around it. For example, a farm community may celebrate its leading crop. Schaller, Iowa, in the middle of a corn-growing region, holds an annual Popcorn Day. Yoakum, Texas, has its Tomato Tom-Tom festival. Memphis, Tennessee, stages a gay and gaudy Cotton Carnival.

Or the holiday may celebrate some natural resource. Hayward, Wisconsin, boasts of the fine fishing thereabout by holding an annual Muskie Carnival in honor of the game fish called the muskellunge. Odessa, Texas, gives thanks for its mineral wealth by holding a yearly Oil Basin Festival. Anchorage, Alaska, pays tribute to its foremost resource with the festival called the Fur Rendezvous.

This sort of thing is not confined to America. Munich, Germany, long famous for its breweries, holds the yearly *Oktoberfest* to celebrate (and advertise) the quality of its beer. Kyoto, Japan, has its annual *Aoi Matsuri*, or "Hollyhock Festival." Quebec, Canada, promotes its winter sports facilities and tourist attractions with a Winter Carnival.

Lourdes, France, is the scene of an almost endless parade, almost every day of the year, because that town has a "natural resource" which is most unusual and, according to Roman Catholic believers, truly a miraculous one. This is a small spring of water in a rock grotto, where

KYOTO, JAPAN, *to celebrate its outstanding local feature of attraction, every year holds the* Aoi Matsuri, *or "Hollyhock Festival," complete with this parade of flower-covered, ox-drawn floats.*

(JAPAN NATL. TOURIST ASSN.)

A RIVER OF CANDLELIGHT *is the effect produced in this time-exposure photograph of the procession at Lourdes, France. What you're seeing is a parade of pilgrims, each bearing a candle, on their way to bathe in the waters of the Lourdes grotto.*

once the Virgin Mary was supposedly seen. Thousands upon thousands of ill and crippled people from all over the world make their pilgrimage to the town and go in procession to the grotto spring, in hopes that a dip in its waters will cure their ailments.

One Italian city used to claim an entire sea as its private resource, and every year—until quite recent times—it staged a distinctive sort of parade to re-stake that claim. The ceremony, known as The Marriage of the Adriatic, took place in the harbor of Venice, that famous city built on water-filled canals instead of streets.

Every Ascension Day (the fortieth day after Easter) a tremendous gondola set out from St. Mark's Square. Gorgeously decorated, it was

ONE-OF-A-KIND *is the indoor parade held in Swedish homes on St. Lucia's Day (December 13). Early in the morning, the children of the house (one playing St. Lucia in a candle crown) march from room to room, waking their elders with song and serving them coffee and "Lucia rolls."*
(SWEDISH NATL. TOURIST OFFICE)

propelled by forty rowers, carried a bevy of priests and the Doge of Venice (the city's chief magistrate). It was followed by a whole fleet of other gondolas, sailing vessels, and barges, carrying lesser officials and priests, deckloads of spectators and music-making minstrels. When the fleet arrived at the offshore island of Lido, in the Adriatic Sea, the Doge performed his traditional ceremony. He poured holy water into the sea, then took from his finger a gold wedding ring and dropped that too into the waves, with the words, "We wed thee, O Sea, in token of our just and perpetual dominion." The idea was that, for another year, the Venetian sailors and fishermen would find the sea as kind, generous, and submissive as a human bride.

A PARADE OF GONDOLAS *on the canals of modern Venice is a reminder of the one-time "Marriage of the Adriatic" ceremony—which must have looked much like this.*
(BROWN BROTHERS)

That Venice ceremony was repeated for seven hundred years before it died out. But die out it did, as most parade days eventually do, when they're based on some purely human notion or perishable commodity. The Odessa Oil Basin Festival, for instance, will someday have to be abandoned, when the Texas oilfields run dry. Even patriotic holidays, though they may seem securely fixed in the calendar, are often dismayingly short-lived. Heroes get forgotten, great victories are overshadowed by later victories (or defeats), and even the country doing the celebrating may disappear from the map. Only the seasonal celebrations, such as Midsummer Day, seem to endure eternally, while whole nations, religions, and civilizations—with all their special holidays— come into being, strut briefly on parade, and fade and disappear.

Ask any New Yorker today, "Whatever became of Evacuation Day?" and chances are he won't know what you're talking about. But, until just a hundred years ago, that was the city's biggest and gayest patriotic holiday. Parades were chockablock in the streets, free barbecues roasted on every corner, and rum and cider flowed like water. What the city celebrated was the anniversary of November 25, 1783, that day at the end of the Revolution when the last defeated British troops sailed out of New York and the American flag flew over the city for the first time.

Of the many other parades that have been long disbanded, one that no one regrets losing was the annual Pope-Burning in the England of Queen Elizabeth I. At that time, the Roman Catholic Church had been outlawed and was hated by most Englishmen. So every November 17, the anniversary of Elizabeth's taking the throne, London would see great processions of people making fun of everything Catholic. Floats and masqueraders depicted the Pope arm-in-arm with the devil, nuns in various ridiculous poses, priests torturing accused witches, etc. The centerpiece of each parade was a giant image of the Pope, with a bag of gunpowder in its belly, and each procession ended with this statue being burned and blown to bits.

These parades and other persecutions of the Catholics had been going on for many years when, in 1605, a few Catholic Englishmen decided to strike a blow for their religious liberty by blowing up Parliament's House of Lords. Fortunately, the plot was discovered—on November 5 of that year—before it could be carried out. The conspirators were all executed or exiled, but the "Gunpowder Plot" so shocked the English people that they detested Catholics all the more. November 5 became Guy Fawkes Day—named after one of the plotters—and the people celebrated the day every year afterward by burning images of both the Pope *and* Guy Fawkes.

GUY FAWKES *plays his usual unhappy part in the parades—this one sketched in 1831—that still march through English streets every November 5th.*

In time, England changed its official attitude and granted Catholics the right to worship in their own way. The common people became ashamed of their Pope-Burnings and stopped having them. Although Guy Fawkes Day is still observed, it has become a holiday mainly for small children, celebrated with costume parades, fireworks, and the bonfire executions of homemade straw "Guys."

However, before the custom of Pope-Burning was abandoned in England, it had crossed the ocean to become a parade day in the English colonies of Massachusetts and New Hampshire. The holiday continued to be celebrated, with the name of Pope Day, even long after the colonies had become the United States. But eventually the Americans forgot the origin of the observance. By the 1800's the name had been slurred to *Pork* Day, and the people assumed that it must be a celebration of the autumn time for slaughtering hogs. Later still, that holiday was merged into the harvest-time Thanksgiving.

But there were other once-upon-a-time parades that it *would* be fun to watch again; for example, the Butcher's Leap and Cooper's Dance that used to be held in Munich, Germany. It seems that the city was ravaged by a dreadful plague, back in the year 1517—and even after it was over the people were afraid to venture out of their houses. To show them that there was no more risk of infection, and to get the city on the go again, the local butchers and coopers (barrel-makers) tempted them out by staging a merry parade. They marched through the streets to the main square, where the coopers did a dance around the central fountain and the butchers gaily jumped *into* it.

This event was commemorated for nearly five hundred years thereafter, the coopers doing their dance every seven years and the butchers repeating their leap every three. It didn't fade away until the 1890's, and in its later occasions it was made part of the graduation ceremony for apprentices in those two trades. The butchers or the coopers, depending on whose turn it was, would parade to the fountain with their boy apprentices in tow. There they would all drink a toast to the royal family. Then the masters would quiz the apprentices on how well they'd learned their trade. When the youngsters had proved themselves worthy to be called masters of their trade, they would complete the ceremony by leaping fully-clothed into the fountain.

Other traditional parades are still with us, though, and some of them are so old that the paraders have forgotten exactly what they are celebrating or what their actions are supposed to symbolize. Consider The Procession of the Herring, which has been repeated annually in the city of Reims, France, since the sixteenth century. On the Wednesday before every Easter, all the priests of the Reims Cathedral march across the city to services at the Church of St. Remi. They walk two by two, and each priest trails behind him a herring on a string. Each marcher's object is to tread on the fish of the man ahead, but prevent his own herring from being stepped on by the man behind. If the priests do still remember what inspired this curious parade, they're not telling outsiders.

Then there's the even older Dance of St. Willibrod, held every year on the seventh Tuesday after Easter in the town of Echternach, Luxembourg. But this one at least has a legend for its inspiration. Nearly six hundred years ago, says the tale, all the cattle of the region were seized by a strange disease that caused them to *dance* themselves to death. The people were in danger of losing every cow they owned, but then good St. Willibrod came along and cured the plague. Now, six centuries later, the peasants still imitate the "cows' dance" in honor of the saint.

Old people, young people, even mothers with babes in arms, all the people from miles around, come to Echternach on this day. They dance

THE DANCE OF ST. WILLIBROD *is here performed by the tots of Echternach, Luxembourg. This curious parade has been danced every year for the past six centuries.*

(INSTITUT GRAND DUCAL, LUXEMBOURG / JEAN WEYRICH)

through the streets to the local church, make an offering at the altar and dance out again. The dance they do is a sort of shuffle—five steps forward, three backward; three steps forward, two back—and so on, repeated over and over. The accompanying music is a polka rhythm that dates back to the fourteenth century. And here's a curiosity. Some music scholars claim that the St. Willibrod tune was the original of the music to the British national anthem "God Save the Queen" (and from which was copied the tune of "America: My County, 'Tis of Thee").

Two Italian cities still hold celebrations that date back to the era of knights in armor. Siena's Race for the Palio recalls the medieval Age of Chivalry, while Arezzo's Joust of the Saracen began even farther back, with the Crusades of the thirteenth century.

The Siena race, a contest among the champion horsemen of ten of the city's districts, takes place every July. The winner's prize is the *palio,* a magnificent black-and-gold banner with a heavy fringe. Before the race, a medieval procession marches around the cobblestoned square called the Piazza del Campo. The parade consists of mace-bearers, the districts' officials, their champion horsemen, pages, drummers, and trumpeters, all in antique costumes. Standard-bearers toss and twirl heavy silk banners bearing the insignia—unicorn, dragon, snail, etc.—of the ten districts. A team of white oxen pulls a carriage from which flies the *palio*.

After the parade, the ten horsemen run their race—several circuits of the piazza—each jockey beating at his own horse, at the other horses (and at the other jockeys) with his *nerbo*, or "stinging whip." The winner is paraded once more around the piazza on the shoulders of the crowd, and then the celebrants and spectators drift off to their home districts for banquets and parties that go on all night long.

Arezzo's Joust, held every September, is preceded by a costumed parade much like the one in Siena. But the Arezzo celebrants, instead of a race, hold a horseback tournament against a wooden dummy that represents the Saracen, the ancient Crusaders' enemy. A long lance securely braced under his arm, each horseman gallops across a field and attempts to spear the dummy. If he hits it just right, he then must try to avoid getting hit in turn, as the "Saracen" is whirled around by the blow and slashes at him with a wicked whip.

THE RACE FOR THE PALIO *at Siena, Italy, is preceded by a parade of flag-tossers, heralds, and armored knights, all in medieval costumes.*

(ITALIAN STATE TOURIST OFFICE)

THE JOUST OF THE SARACEN *at Arezzo, Italy, is a contest between armored knight-crusaders like these, seen parading before the joust, and a wooden dummy "Saracen" mounted on a pole.*
(ITALIAN STATE TOURIST OFFICE)

The *Festa dos Tabuleiros,* or "Festival of the Trays," held in the town of Tomar, Portugal, is such an ancient ceremony that no one knows *when* it began. The best guess is that it was inspired by the Romans' celebration in honor of Ceres, goddess of the harvest—in which case it dates back some two thousand years, to the time when Roman legions occupied this country.

The Festival of Trays is held during the second week in July, but only in odd-numbered years (1967, 1969, 1971, etc.). It takes its name from the odd headdresses that the Tomar girls wear during the festival's main parade. Six hundred girls march at one time, each of them balancing on her head a construction that *must,* by tradition, be "as tall as the girl who wears it." Directly atop her head she has a round wicker tray, and built onto that is a high framework of bamboo and wire. On this are hung exactly thirty loaves of bread, and the whole affair—which may weigh more than thirty pounds—is topped with a cross or a toy dove with an olive branch in its beak. After the parade, the loaves of bread are blessed by a priest and then are distributed among the poor. But no one eats it, no matter how poor or hungry he may be. Each family keeps its loaf in the belief that it brings good luck—though if someone gets ill, he may take a bite of the bread for medicine.

There are many more of these one-of-a-kind parades, each of which is peculiar to a single community. There's the happy Festival of King Pumpkin, held in Les Halles, the market district of Paris, when the largest pumpkin of the harvest is given a tinsel crown, paraded on a wooden throne, and later is made into pumpkin soup to be shared by every worker in the markets. There's the gloomy Procession of the Penitents, observed for the past nine hundred years in Furnes, Belgium, when crowds of barefooted men and women, clad all in black, imitate the last moments of Jesus Christ by staggering through the streets, each bent under a massive wooden cross. There's the horrible parade held every May in Karachi, India, to mourn the murder—thirteen centuries ago—of the Caliph Imam Hussain. Some ten thousand Moslem men and boys parade, naked to the waist, flailing themselves with knives and chains so that they cover the streets with their blood.

But there have been other parades even more distinctive and individual, because each of them was performed just *once*, and never again. For example, there was the all-nude parade held at St. Denis, France, in the spring of the year 1315. The farmlands thereabout had been desolated for weeks by a steady deluge of rain and sleet, so the people decided to mortify themselves in hopes that heaven would take pity on them. Men, women, and children came to the town "from five leagues around," stripped to the skin and marched through the streets carrying crosses and other religious objects. There is no record of whether the weather improved.

ANOTHER ONE-OF-A-KIND parade is *the Perchtenlauf, held every fourth year in the Gastein Valley of Austria. The marchers in their antique costumes and skyscraper headdresses represent the forces of Good and Evil. (Note that the "female" paraders are impersonated by men.)*
(AUSTRIAN INFORMATION SERVICE)

There was the all-woman parade held in New York City in 1915. This was a "demonstration march" by the women known as suffragettes, who were demanding the right to vote (a right which women didn't have in all of the United States in those days). Fifty thousand of them, each wearing across her breast the yellow sash that was the suffragettes' badge, marched down Fifth Avenue that morning. Five years later, all the women of all the states got their right to vote.

The discovery or invention of some new thing has often been greeted by a parade whose like is never seen again. Only one "Columbus Day," for instance, has ever included a parade led by Christopher Columbus himself. It took place in Barcelona, Spain, in 1493, when he returned from discovering the New World, and it celebrated his being given the title of "Admiral of the Ocean Sea." Columbus led the procession on a white horse, flanked by King Ferdinand and Prince Charles. Behind them marched the crew of the good ship Niña (the only one of Columbus's three vessels that made it back to Spain). The sailors carried the souvenirs of the voyage—parrots, popinjays, and a few small animals.

THIS ALL-WOMAN PARADE *of Suffragettes "demonstrated" on New York's Fifth Avenue in 1915, to demand that every American woman be given the right to vote.*

(BROWN BROTHERS)

Also in the parade were six rather bewildered Indians whom Columbus had persuaded to come home with him. They supposedly marched in their "native costumes," but actually, since their customary costume was practically nothing at all, Columbus had to make the Indians put on extra clothes to be "decent" for the parade.

Even the start of what might be called the Automobile Age had its welcoming parade. In 1899 the "horseless carriage" was still quite a novel invention, and few people but the wealthy could afford to own one. So it's no surprise that the 1899 parade saluting the automobile was dreamed up by a group of rich women in the "high society" resort town of Newport, Rhode Island. For the occasion, they dressed their cars all over with fresh flowers: along the sides, around the wheel rims, along the runningboards. The cars' open bodies (there were no closed cars in those days) wore high arches of flowers like the hoops of a covered wagon. Among the blossoms perched artificial birds and butterflies, and long ribbons streamed from radiator caps and wheel hubs. Although, with all these trimmings, no vehicle in the procession *looked* like an automobile, this was still the first all-automobile parade ever staged.

There's another sort of parade that is one-of-a-kind—not because it is limited to any one locality or any special day, but because it's the one parade that just about everybody marches in, soon or later, and generally only once in his or her lifetime.

This is the wedding procession, familiar to practically every community on earth. In this country, the typical church wedding usually includes a total of three processions. First there's the slow-paced march of the bride down the aisle to the altar, preceded by her flower girls, ring-bearing page, bridesmaids, etc. This is essentially a fashion parade, to show off her wedding gown and her attendants' costumes to the ooh-ing and aah-ing ladies in the congregation. After the ceremony, there's the rather quicker-paced march of the bride and bridegroom out of the church, ducking through a shower of thrown rice and confetti. Then there's the motorcade of automobiles that carries the wedding party away from the church, with horns blaring to proclaim the joyous occasion.

Although the wedding program is now done according to rules of procedure as formal as those of a chess game, and is regarded as the highest expression of civilized taste and etiquette, it actually contains elements of tradition and superstition that date back to the Stone Age. In those days, a man who wanted a mate had to kidnap her from another tribe. The people of today who gaily throw rice and whatnot at the newly-married couple are simply imitating the Stone Age tribesmen

THE WORLD'S BEST-KNOWN *once-in-a-lifetime parade is the wedding procession —though it's not always as picturesque as this ceremony in Hamburg, Germany, complete with page boys, flower girls, white horses, and "Cinderella" coach.*
(GERMAN INFORMATION CENTER)

who threw spears and rocks at the kidnapper-bridegroom as he escaped with their young woman. The rice that is thrown is a leftover from an old superstition—that to pelt a new couple with any kind of grain would make them as fruitful as the grain itself, and insure a good "harvest" of children. The horn-blowing motorcade is a modern-day survival of another old belief—that evil demons lurked around any happy occasion, ready to do mischief, and had to be frightened off by noisemakers.

But, despite these touches of antique color, the weddings in our country are rather pale and tame compared to the sometimes curious marriage customs in other places. In many parts of the world, especially in rural peasant communities, the bridegroom still plays the "cave man," leading a troop of his friends in a kidnap raid on the bride's house or village. Nowadays, of course, her family and neighbors willingly cooperate in giving the girl away. But sometimes the kidnapping is acted-out to the extent of having a mock-battle between her people and his. Anyway, he and his "best men" eventually carry her off in a triumphal procession. And several communities, though widely separated—in Scandinavia and India, for instance—have the same tradition: that the carrying-off must be done on a white horse.

In other places, the man often has to "buy" his wife. And so, when he makes his formal visit to her family to ask for her hand in marriage, he comes at the head of a whole parade of his kinfolk, all loaded down with gifts, leading cows or bringing whatever other sort of currency is the standard purchase price. This is still a custom in countries as far apart as Bulgaria and the Congo.

Among the Koryaks of northeastern Asia, the bridegroom goes to his wedding dressed as a woman and the bride goes dressed as a man. This mixup is supposed to confuse the evil demons so that they won't bother either one. In parts of Russia, it is still the custom for the bride, or the whole wedding procession, to shuffle along draped with a huge fishing net, because a fishing net is a mass of knots and evil spirits are believed helpless to untie the knots and get at the people.

A SWEDISH BRIDE AND BRIDEGROOM *dress up in old-time native garb for their wedding. Here and in other countries, the custom is for the husband to provide a white horse for the procession to and from the church.*

(SWEDISH NATL. TRAVEL OFFICE)

IN A KOREAN WEDDING PROCESSION, *the bridegroom proudly leads the march mounted on a shaggy pony, while his bride (looking a trifle uneasy) follows in a litter-chair borne by the "best men."*
(EMBASSY OF KOREA)

Probably the slowest and most complicated wedding parade in the world is that held in some parts of Portugal. On its way to the church, the wedding party has to pass under three arches, each covered with flowers and hung with the symbols of husband-and-wifely duties. Hanging from the first arch is a distaff (the spindle from a spinning wheel), a pen, ink, and paper. The bride-to-be takes up the distaff and spins a few strands of thread; her husband-to-be takes the pen and writes a few words. A little farther down the road, the procession comes to the second arch, where hang a book and a pillow. The man reads a few words while the girl embroiders a few stitches on the pillow. After another short march, the parade reaches the third arch, hung with a stocking and a sword. The girl does a bit of darning on the stocking; the man slashes about with the sword in "defense" of his mate. Having had this brief introduction to "married life," the young couple can now go on to the church ceremony, and begin the real thing.

V

Hail the Conquering Hero

THE KIND OF PARADE THAT we guess to have been the "first ever"—that triumphal celebration at the cavemen's return from the hunt—has marched countless times since then, and still is staged today, whenever a hero comes home, or visits somewhere, or takes his place in high office.

The Bible mentions several triumphal parades. The Old Testament Book of Esther tells of the one staged in Persia in the fifth century B.C. to honor Mordecai for having saved King Ahasuerus's life: "Then took Haman the apparel and the horse, and arrayed Mordecai, and brought him on horseback through the street of the city, and proclaimed before him, Thus shall it be done unto the man whom the king delighteth to honor." The New Testament Book of Matthew describes Jesus Christ's entry into Jerusalem. Although Jesus arrived without much fanfare, and riding on a humble donkey: "a very great multitude spread their garments in the way; others cut down branches from the trees, and strewed them in the way. And the multitudes that went before, and that followed, cried, saying Hosanna to the son of David . . ."

About the same time, the Romans were holding their frequent and lavish triumphal receptions for the legions returning from conquests in far places. On the other side of the world, the Aztecs and Incas of Central and South America held equally magnificent ceremonies at the coronations of their god-emperors. In the jungles of Africa and the frozen deserts of Siberia, even the smallest and most insignificant tribes mustered whatever shabby splendor they could, to salute the succession of a new chieftain or witch-doctor.

A HERO'S WELCOME *is depicted in this drawing of the "Battle of Love" staged at Florence, Italy, in 1631 to honor the visiting Grand Duke of Tuscany. The ceremonies included numerous triumphal parades, tableaus, marching exhibitions, concerts, and mock war games.*

In Europe, after the fall of the Roman empire, much of the gaiety and showiness faded out of parades—triumphal and every other kind—and stayed out for a long time. It wasn't until the twelfth century that parades again became lively occasions, and acquired many of the adornments that they couldn't do without today. It was the Crusaders' triumphal homecomings that did it.

When the crusading knights first rode off to the Holy Land to fight the Saracens, they and their horses were impressively heavy with armor and bristly with weapons. But their going-away parades were strictly businesslike; no fun to them. When they came back from the Crusades, however, they brought something new and different in the way of parades.

The Crusaders had learned a few tricks from their Saracen enemies; for one thing, how to use music for military purposes. So their homecoming parades marched to music—and the music was played on all sorts of new and interesting instruments. Over their grim armor the knights now wore colorful, flowing robes and rakish turbans. And in their triumphal parades marched their captured slaves, black Moors and brown Arabs seldom seen before in Europe.

All these novelties—the costumes, the music, the vivid splashes of color—have been part of the western world's parades ever since. Even the slaves still march, in a way. Because, long after the Crusade era, every parade still had to have its "blackamoors." These were played by clowns in blackface makeup, and this is what started the idea of parading in masks and grotesque disguises.

Since the Crusaders put new life into it, the triumphal reception has often shown twice the glitter and glamour of any other parade occasion. Because there is not only the parade itself, with its marchers, bands, floats, costumes, and whatever else; the spectators get into the act, too. They decorate the streets and buildings, sometimes even themselves, and strive to put on the best possible show for the guest or guests of honor.

On November 23, 1415, when England's King Henry V returned from the Battle of Agincourt and his victory over the French, London received him like this:

As soon as he and his parade of troops entered the city, tremendous flocks of white doves were let fly from the rooftops and fluttered "thikke about the kyng." All the fountains in the city spouted wine that day instead of water. Boys dressed in white skipped along behind the king's white horse and threw gold coins to the crowd. At one street corner stood a high wooden castle, newly built for the occasion, in the arches of which perched two dozen white-bearded old men. According to a chronicle of the time, the ancients represented "twelve aposteles syngyng, twelve kynges knelyng." While singing and kneeling, the apostles and kings tossed out little silver disks that symbolized the holy wafers of the Communion service. At London Bridge, the parade passed under two giant statues of the British lion and unicorn. From the walls of St. Paul's Cathedral, a group of lovely girls, all in white, scattered leaves of gold down onto the procession. At another street corner stood another imitation castle; from its windows leaned a chorus of girls, playing on tambourines and singing, "Welcome to the Fifth Henry, King of England and of France!"

Five centuries later, British royalty was still enjoying similar pageantry. When King George V and Queen Mary decided to visit the colony of India, and set the date for December, 1911, the Indian people began preparing for their *durbar* (reception) a whole year ahead of time. Twenty-five square miles of sandy desert outside the capital city of Delhi were plowed, irrigated, planted, and transformed into trim green lawns and blooming gardens. Great pavilions of carved wood, silk, and ivory were erected, together with an amphitheater to seat ten thousand. But that was scarcely finished when the durbar committee decided it would be far too small. So laborers were put to work carrying basket after basket of earth until they had piled up an artificial mountain on which fifty thousand more spectators could stand.

An English colonial official, who was there, described the durbar as "the supreme moment of triumph, beside which the glories of ancient Rome may be thought to pale." The king and queen, wearing their crowns and ermine robes, rode in a carriage at the head of the parade as it entered the amphitheater, then were enthroned in the place of honor to watch the procession pass in review.

Cannons on the parade ground roared a salute that was echoed, after a moment, by other guns miles away in the hills. Dozens of bands played, one after another. The welcoming parade included a hundred corps of troops—just about every military unit in the country, of both the British and Indian armies. Afoot or on superb horses, their swords and lances flashing and clashing, came the hussars in brilliant blue, the dragoons in royal scarlet, the lancers in ornamental armored breastplates, the Indian troops in many-colored turbans and fierce black beards. Besides the soldiers, there were marchers in the parade who were rulers in their own right. The Maharajahs of Kashmir and Mysore, the Gaekwar of Baroda, the Nizam of Hyderabad—these and all the other ruling chiefs of India stepped down from their own thrones on this occasion to pay homage to Their Britannic Majesties.

But triumphal celebrations, like other sorts of parades, don't always come off so smoothly. Some of the best-intentioned ceremonies of welcome have been spoiled by an embarrassing situation or even a disaster.

In the year 1066, William of Normandy invaded and conquered what was then Saxon England, and in due course presented himself at London's Westminster Abbey to be crowned King William I. Crowds of Londoners gathered at the Abbey gates to watch the coronation procession and, even though this new king had forced himself upon them, the Englishmen were good sports enough to cheer as the parade passed. However, cheering was a Saxon custom, and William's soldiers had never heard such a thing back in Normandy. They thought the crowd was shouting a war-cry and getting ready to attack the king. So the soldiers rode straight into the mob, trampling people under their horses' hooves and whacking at them with maces and battle-axes. A good many innocent bystanders were killed and maimed. In the milling confusion, a number of household hearth fires got scattered, set ablaze the

A TRIUMPHAL ARCH *is usually a feature of any triumphal parade. This one was erected by the gunmakers' guild of Birmingham, England, to welcome the visiting Queen Victoria.*

thatched buildings in the neighborhood and nearly burned down Westminster Abbey itself.

In 1572, when Queen Elizabeth I made a visit to Warwick Castle, the Earl of Warwick had waiting for her a midnight reception featuring a special surprise. This was supposed to be "a Dragon flieng, casting out huge flames and squibes." It was evidently some sort of rocket-and-firecracker contraption, and the plan was that it would fly through the sky, crash into an imitation fortress on the castle grounds and blow it up. But something went wrong. The dragon whizzed over Elizabeth's head, in the wrong direction, and disappeared into the night. Somewhat later, the disappointed earl got news that it had landed in the middle of town, on the house of a Mr. and Mrs. Henry Cooper, who were asleep in bed at the time and not expecting dragons. It had set fire to their thatched roof and the Coopers had nearly perished before their astonished neighbors could break in and rescue them.

Sometimes the guest of honor just can't survive his triumphal celebration. In 1377, when Richard II was crowned King of England, he had to endure a three-hour parade from the Tower of London to Westminster Abbey. Everywhere there were crowds, musicians, triumphal arches to be admired. At one corner was erected a castle covered all over with silver leather. From each of its four turrets a maiden showered the new king with golden leaves and coins. From the central dome an "angel" (another girl, painted from head to foot with gold) floated down on a sort of crane arrangement, placed a gilt crown on the king's head and offered him wine from a golden cup. Finally the procession arrived at the Abbey and, after the coronation ceremony—itself a long, tedious, and fatiguing business—the king was supposed to retrace his earlier street parade. But he had completely given out. So—"contrary to ancient custom," a spectator reported, "and the Abbot of the place protesting"—his faithful servant, Sir Simon Burley, simply picked up the king, in all his royal robes and jewels, and carried him all the way home, asleep on his shoulder. King Richard, you see, was only ten years old at the time.

THE STATE OPENING OF PARLIAMENT *in London is celebrated with a grand parade every time the Members of Parliament meet in session.*
(BRITISH TRAVEL ASSOCIATION)

There are parades at kings' coronations, at presidents' inaugurations, at popes' assumptions. But all of these are far between and total just a few, in comparison to the triumphal parade that ushers into office the Lord Mayor of London.

(You remember the story of Dick Whittington; how the church bells rang out to stop the discouraged lad from leaving the city. They seemed to chant, "Turn again, Dick Whittington—thou'lt be Lord Mayor of London town!" Well, there really *was* a Dick Whittington, and he really did become Lord Mayor of London—three times, in the years 1397, 1406, and 1419.)

The Lord Mayor's Show has been held almost every year since the city's first mayor took office in 1192. In Dick Whittington's time, the parade was entirely water-borne. Indeed, in those days, almost every London celebration had to do its parading on the Thames River, because the city streets were so narrow and their open sewers were so filthy.

The centerpiece of the water parade was the Lord Mayor's Barge, a beautifully shaped and ornamented boat that looked like something Cleopatra might have lolled in. It flew flags and pennants with "little belles at ye endes whiche made a goodly noyse." Besides the new Lord Mayor himself, it carried the parade's "mynstrelsie," or band of musi-

A **FLOTILLA OF STATE BARGES** *on the Thames, to celebrate the building of a new London bridge in the nineteenth century, makes up a parade that very much resembles the water-borne Lord Mayor's Shows of three hundred years earlier.*

(N.Y. PUBLIC LIBRARY)

cians, with "all its drumes and flutes and trumpettes blohyng." The rest of the parade consisted of the barges built by the city's various trade guilds—the Grocers, Ironmongers, Goldsmiths, and so on. The barge paraded by the Worshipful Company of Clothworkers one year was decorated with three life-size, carved, gold-plated sheep atop its cabin. Besides vying with each other to build the most original and handsomest barge, the guilds were forever squabbling about which of them should be ahead of others in the river procession. It is recorded that, in 1483, the Merchant Tailors and the Skinners came to blows over this, and one man was killed.

Later, when London had been cleaned up considerably, the Lord Mayor's Show moved onto the streets, and the guilds built floats instead of barges. The Fishmongers' float of 1700 represented a sailing ship manned by "some Men and Boys in it, drawing of a Net, in which came up a great many live Fish, which they flung among the Livery-men." Another year, the Merchant Tailors' contribution to the parade was simply a man and woman marching side by side—Adam and Eve, wearing their traditional fig leaves—as a humorous indication of how long, long ago the ".tailoring business" got its start.

In the seventeenth century, celebrities in the various fields of art were invited to lend their talents in the planning of the Lord Mayor's Show. Several of the parades were produced by Thomas Middleton, a playwright who was nearly as popular as that other author of the period, William Shakespeare. The show which Middleton arranged for 1613 had the Lord Mayor involved with a whole cast of masquerade characters representing the virtues, such as Truth, Justice, Wisdom, doing battle with such vices as Error and Envy.

The show no longer makes such a heavy-handed attempt to teach the Lord Mayor how to behave in his high post. Nor does London go to great lengths any more to dress up the whole town for the occasion. But the Lord Mayor's Show still is held, and it hasn't changed much in the last three or four hundred years. The Lord Mayor still rides in a beautiful, gilded, six-horse coach, and all the soldiers, warders, and aldermen wear Elizabethan uniforms and costumes. Dick Whittington might not feel at home in this year's parade, but Thomas Middleton would.

Of all the sorts of triumphal celebrations practiced today, probably the best known is New York City's traditional "ticker-tape" parade. New York has always been eager and lavish with its hospitality to visiting celebrities. Why, back at the beginning of the American Revolution, the city folk even turned out twice on the same day to pay tribute to representatives of *both* the warring nations.

It happened in 1775, just a week after the Battle of Bunker Hill and

two weeks after George Washington had been named commander-in-chief of the Continental forces. On the morning of June 27, Washington came through New York on his way to take command of his troops outside Boston. All the American sympathizers in New York (plus everybody else who enjoyed a parade) came out in crowds to cheer as he rode by. That afternoon, the British-appointed colonial governor of New York, William Tryon, returned from a visit to England, and all the British sympathizers in the city (plus everybody else who enjoyed a parade) came out in crowds to welcome him home.

After the Revolution, in 1788, Alexander Hamilton helped to organize a city parade in honor of the newly-written United States Constitution. All the working men of the city turned out to march. The blacksmiths contributed a horse-drawn float that carried a real fire and a working forge. As it rolled along they hammered out a real anchor on the anvil. The bakers tossed buns to the spectators. The printers' float carried a real printing press that stamped out copies of a poem written in praise of the new Constitution, and the sheets of paper were thrown to the crowd as fast as they were printed. The parade's finale was the *Ship of State,* a war frigate under full canvas, carrying thirty sailors and

THE "SHIP OF STATE" *fires a salute, during New York's 1788 parade in honor of the newly-written United States Constitution.*

drawn by ten horses. When the parade ended up at Bowling Green on lower Broadway, the ship fired off a thirteen-gun salute to the thirteen states.

New York has celebrated all kinds of other American triumphs. When the Erie Canal opened in 1825, connecting the Hudson River and the Great Lakes, a parade of forty-six vessels sailed from Lake Erie, through the Canal, down the Hudson, through New York harbor and out into the Atlantic Ocean. The steamships, barges, pilot boats, canal-boats, and revenue cutters steamed into a circle three miles in diameter, while Governor DeWitt Clinton emptied a keg of Lake Erie water into the Atlantic waves to symbolize the "marriage of the waters."

In 1919, as the American soldiers began coming home after World War I, the regiments marched up New York's Fifth Avenue in one triumphal procession after another. At Sixtieth Street, each parade passed under a massive "Arch of Jewels" that had cost $40,000 to erect. It was built of 30,000 pieces of different-colored crystal embedded in white plaster, and bore the coats-of-arms of all the Allied nations.

But New York's most distinctive triumphal celebration got its start back in 1824. The Marquis de Lafayette, a French nobleman who had fought under Washington during the Revolution, was making his first visit to America since the war, and New York gave him a hero's welcome. The parade met him as he stepped off his ship at the Battery (New York's waterfront) and carried him between crowds of cheering spectators, up Broadway to City Hall to be formally greeted by Mayor Stephen Allen. This is the same route—from the Battery up Broadway to City Hall—that almost all of New York's welcome parades have taken since then. And the stretch of lower Broadway that they pass through has long been the city's financial district. Every office there used to contain a telegraph "ticker" machine that kept the businessmen instantly informed of changes in the stock market by printing a continuous stream of stock prices on "ticker tape." As this paper tape unrolled and inched out of the machine, it was collected in waste baskets and thrown away. Or it was until one day in 1899.

That day, New York staged a triumphal welcome for Admiral George Dewey, in honor of his victory over the Spanish Navy in the Battle of Manila Bay. Perhaps some office boy in one of the tall Broadway buildings was emptying waste baskets when the parade came by, and it occurred to him that ticker tape would make a dandy substitute for confetti. At any rate, *somebody* threw out a tangle of ticker tape, and people in other buildings followed suit.

At each new parade after that, the fall of ticker tape increased until—at the 1927 welcome-home parade for Charles A. Lindbergh after his historic solo flight across the Atlantic—the paper fall became a blizzard. Since then, every time the city's Sanitation Department sweeps up after a parade, it weighs the result, and the tonnage of ticker tape is some measure of that hero's popularity. Lindbergh rated 1,750 tons, a record that wasn't broken until 1951, when General Douglas MacArthur returned from the Korean War. His parade was showered with 3,249 tons of tape. Then, in 1962, when astronaut John Glenn rode in triumph up Broadway after his space flight three times around the earth, he set a new ticker-tape record with 3,474 tons.

The ticker-tape parades have greeted military and civilian heroes, sports champions, kings and queens, presidents and prime ministers, emperors and empresses. England's Queen Elizabeth II set the popularity record among foreign visitors; her 1957 parade piled up eight hundred tons of ticker tape. Even one "cultural hero" has been so honored —the American pianist Van Cliburn, when he returned from winning a musical competition in Russia.

The ticker-tape parade is such an unmistakable mark of a visitor's prestige that foreign dignitaries willingly arrange their visits to the United States so as to be sure of receiving one. For example, they'll arrange *not* to arrive in New York on a weekend, when there's no one in the Broadway offices to throw the ticker tape. One South American president, when told that he was too unpopular in the United States to expect a ticker-tape reception, flew into a rage and cancelled his whole trip.

There's no denying that a ticker-tape parade makes a pretty picture. The dark canyons between the building cliffs, from skyscraper peaks to parade level, are snow-thick with the dancing, spiraling, drifting, coiling, unfurling streamers of tape. No other city has ever successfully imitated the parade.

A TICKER-TAPE PARADE, *this one honoring Astronaut John Glenn, makes its way up New York's Broadway through a seeming snowstorm of tape, confetti, and torn paper.*

(WIDE WORLD PHOTOS)

But, in all honesty, it must be reported that ticker-tape parades are not what they used to be. In recent years, the ticker machines have been supplied with a new plastic tape that can be used over and over, and so doesn't get thrown away. On parade occasions, so that people will have something to throw, city government employees must go from office to office handing out packages of old paper ticker tape and cartons of trimmings donated by paper companies. But it's becoming difficult for people to throw even that, because so many of Broadway's new office buildings are air-conditioned and therefore have their windows sealed shut. On recent parade days, the government employees have had to stand on building roofs and setbacks and scatter the ticker tape themselves. A lot of the old-fashioned, unforced enthusiasm has gone out of the parades, and the visitors being honored might feel considerably less important if they realized they were getting such a prearranged hoorah.

Even so, that's better than some of the receptions that visitors have got elsewhere. Quite frequently, and unhappily, triumphal celebrations have *made* history instead of celebrating it. In 1901, President William McKinley visited a world's fair at Buffalo, New York. During his reception, an assassin stepped from the crowd and shot him. The President died eight days later.

A parade-day murder with more far-reaching consequences took place in the city of Sarajevo, Bosnia, in 1914. The visiting Archduke Franz Ferdinand of Austria-Hungary and his wife, Countess Sophie, were riding in their welcome procession when a Serbian assassin shot and killed them both. Austria declared war on Serbia in revenge. Other powers lined up on the side of one country or the other. Before the year was out, all of Europe was up in arms and the First World War was underway.

In our own time, on November 22, 1963, President John F. Kennedy's visit to Dallas, Texas, began with a gala welcome parade and ended just minutes later in a salvo of bullets from an assassin's rifle. That terrible day has not yet dwindled to become just one more dusty date in the history books. Most of us can remember exactly where we were and what we were doing when the shocking news came, and can still feel the horror and hurt we felt then.

Presidents, kings, and other heads of state might be able to avoid such perils by declining to accept invitations anywhere, or at least by not taking part in triumphal processions. But they can hardly refuse to appear at their own inauguration or coronation ceremonies. And here, since the whole idea is to let their fellow citizens get a close look at them, they're almost "sitting duck" targets for any madman in the

AFTER THE PARADE *at Sarajevo in which he was assassinated, Archduke Franz Ferdinand's body is borne homeward to Austria in a far less festive procession.*
(BROWN BROTHERS)

throng. (The typical inauguration parade creeps along at just three miles per hour.)

These days, especially since the Kennedy assassination, well-trained bodyguards try to foresee and forestall any such tragic ending to the ceremonies. The U. S. President's car is completely bulletproof, even the glass top. So is the glassed-in stand where he takes the oath of office. His bodyguards, agents of the Secret Service, won't let anyone watch from a window along the parade route—not even the window's owner—unless he has been carefully checked and approved. Manholes in the parade street are sealed shut for the day, lest an assassin hide himself or a bomb under one of them. And of course all the other people who take part in the inaugural parade are sternly screened and searched. At President Lyndon B. Johnson's 1965 inauguration, a troop of Cochiti Indians danced in the parade. But before they did, the Secret Service men made them remove the arrowheads from the arrows they carried.

VI

Rally Round the Flag

PROBABLY THE MOST TRULY TRIUMPHAL PARADE is a victorious army's return home from war or a campaign of conquest. The welcoming crowds are jubilant enough, just to see their men safe again, but often this sort of parade provides an additional thrill by displaying the treasures, prisoners or other trophies the conquerors have captured from the enemy.

The Plains Indian warriors of North America used to ride home proudly brandishing the scalps of their slain foes. The Jivaro Indians of South America would come back from a raid with their enemies' whole heads, to be shrunken for keepsakes. Though rather less grisly, the homecomings staged by the Roman legions were more spectacular. An eyewitness, the historian Flavius Josephus, left us an account* of one of these parades—the legions' triumphant entry into Rome in the year A.D. 71, after they had put down a revolt in the colony of Judea:

"Almost all the remarkable and valuable objects which have ever been collected were on that day massed together, affording a clear demonstration of the might of the Roman Empire. The quantities of silver, gold, and ivory resembled a running river of wealth. Translucent gems, embedded in diadems or other objects, were borne in such profusion as to dispel any idea that they were rare. Images of the Roman gods passed by, wonderfully big and very skillfully worked, all of them made of expensive materials. Many kinds of beasts were led along, all with their individual trappings. In charge of each part of the procession was a number of men in purple and gold costumes. Even the prisoners

---

* Condensed from B. K. Workman's translation in his book *They Saw It Happen in Classical Times* (Oxford: Basil Blackwell, 1964, and New York: Barnes and Noble, 1964) pp. 157-58.

were worth seeing—no disordered mob, the variety and beauty of their clothes diverted the eye from the disfigurement of their injuries.

"The greatest amazement was caused by the floats. Their size gave grounds for alarm about their stability, for many were three or four storeys high, an astonishing and pleasurable sight. Many were covered in cloth of gold, and worked gold or ivory was fixed on all of them. The craftsmanship and magnificence of the tableaus gave to those who had not witnessed the events as clear an idea of them as if they had been present. Here was a fertile land being ravaged; here whole detachments of enemy being slaughtered, others in flight and others being led off into captivity. Here were walls of colossal size being pounded down by siege-engines; here strongpoints being captured; and here well-defended fortifications overwhelmed. On one float the army could be seen pouring inside the walls; on another was a place running with blood. Others showed defenseless men raising their hands in entreaty, firebrands being hurled at temples or buildings falling on their owners. On yet others were depicted rivers, which, after the destruction and desolation, flowed no longer through tilled fields, but through a land on fire from end to end."

A more recent triumphal procession was far less festive than the Romans', but, in its grim and angry way, it told just as dramatically of an enemy's total vanquishment. It took place in 1945, at the close of World War II, in the Russian capital of Moscow.

It was a day of pouring rain, as bleak as the ceremony to come. Red Square's vast cobblestoned plain was cold and shining wet under ugly gray clouds, but it was crowded with people when the parade marched in. There was no music; just the muffled beat of a drum and the slow tramp of heavy boots. There was no cheering; the crowd was solemn and silent as the procession crossed the square to the reviewing stand, where waited the Russian premier, Josef Stalin. Every soldier in the parade carried a flag—not a Russian but a *German* flag, drooping and bedraggled. There were regimental banners, battle standards, the red-and-black swastika flags—all the German flags that these troops had captured during the last months of the war.

In silence, each rank of soldiers halted before the reviewing stand, dipped its flags in salute and then hurled them to the wet pavement at Stalin's feet. The soldiers wheeled to the right and marched away, while another rank took their place to repeat the action. Then another rank, and another. By the end of that gray day—when the parade was over, the crowd gone, and the square empty—the rain beat down onto a sodden hill of flags, once victorious and haughty, now forever defeated and disgraced.

A GRIM AND ANGRY PARADE *of 1945 ends in Moscow's Red Square with the Russian soldiers flinging to the pavement the banners of the defeated German Army.*

(SOVFOTO)

Another kind of triumphal parade is an army's march into newly conquered territory. This is seldom a happy occasion. The losers naturally give the parade a glum and hostile reception, and even the winners may feel that the triumph is small reward for the loss of their comrades who died to win it. But sometimes even this kind of parade can be a joyous celebration for all concerned.

The city of Paris was the scene of two different—very different—triumphal parades during World War II. The first occurred on June 14, 1940, when the city fell before the juggernaut onslaught of the German Army. Doubtless the invaders' hearts swelled with pride as they marched in. After all, in taking Paris, these Germans had succeeded where their fathers had failed (in World War I). But their victory parade must have been a disappointment. Marching with the distinctive stiff-legged high kick of the traditional German "goose step," they found themselves advancing through streets that were empty and silent. Almost all the unhappy Frenchmen had shut themselves indoors on this black day, and refused to give the Germans the satisfaction of so much as a glance from their windows.

PARIS, 1940. *Through empty, silent streets, a parade of German occupation troops marches into the newly-conquered city.*
(FRENCH EMBASSY)

Compare that scene with the one four years later, on August 25, 1944, when the Allied forces arrived to set Paris free again. As the German occupation troops made an undignified back-door retreat to the eastward, the first liberators entered the city from the west, and were immediately engulfed by cheering, weeping, laughing crowds of French men, women, and children. Though food and wine had long been scarce in Paris, preciously hoarded stores of them now were broken out, to be pressed upon the first arriving soldiers—together with hearty hugs and happy kisses.

The earliest arrivals were single soldiers or jeeploads of them who had straggled out ahead of their units. The main body of the Allied forces was deliberately held up, outside the city, until it could be composed into marching order. As soon as the advance units had cleared the city of the remaining diehard German snipers, the army of liberation was sent in, bands playing, flags flying, in a grand triumphal parade. Leading it was the 2nd French Armored Division, composed of "Free French" troops who had not surrendered when their country did, but had fled to England to wait until they could fight again. Now they had the honor (and revenge) of accepting the formal surrender of Paris from the defeated German commander.

PARIS, 1944. *Hysterically happy Frenchmen rush to greet the first Allied troops to enter the newly liberated city.*
(FRENCH EMBASSY)

PARIS CELEBRATES ITS LIBERATION *with a sky parade of Free French warplanes. Notice that the first wave is flying in the formation of France's traditional symbol, the Cross of Lorraine.*

(FRENCH EMBASSY)

Except for the rare triumphal parade, soldiers in wartime don't do much parading just for show. They more often march for the very practical purpose of getting from one place to another. Of course, this isn't as frequently necessary as it was in olden times, what with modern planes, trains, and trucks to carry them on the long hauls. But when marching *is* called for, its only resemblance to a parade is that the men are strung out in some formation of column or line. There are no bugles or banners, no fifes or drums. The troops are usually clad in drab field uniforms and slouching miserably, because each man has to carry some sixty pounds of equipment. The marching may have to be done through rain, snow, churned-up mud, suffocating dust, or even under fire from enemy guns. A good part of the parade may consist of wounded men on stretchers or painfully limping and falling behind. And some may not make it all the way to parade's end.

No, that dreary, slogging sort of parade wouldn't look like much alongside a grand triumphal procession. And yet, consider—long after the Roman Empire had fallen and its sensational victory parades had been forgotten, there still remained, crisscrossing all of Europe, the paved roads that the empire had laid down for its unpretty, unglamorous foot soldiers to march along.

In peacetime, though, servicemen take part in all sorts of parades. At almost any large military post, on almost any day, you can watch the parade ceremony of the "changing of the guard." It generally goes something like this:

The troop of sentries who have been on duty for the past twenty-four hours march into formation and await the arrival of the guards who'll replace them on duty. The two formations face each other and present arms in a mutual salute. The new guards are inspected by their commanding officer, who selects the man with the neatest uniform and best cared-for weapon to be his personal runner. Then the new guards are marched to their posts, while the old guards parade away in dismissal. This ceremony takes a good half-hour or longer, and is done with movements as traditional and patterned as a minuet, usually accompanied by the music of a brass band.

Probably no tourist visitor to London has ever neglected to take snapshots of the changing of the Royal Guard at Buckingham Palace, the most famous and popular of such exhibitions. But ceremonies just as impressive can be seen on this side of the Atlantic—for example, at the Arlington National Cemetery in Virginia, and at the Citadel in Quebec, Canada (where the fort's mascot, a handsome white goat with gilded horns, marches in the guards' parade).

The most massive and elaborate sort of military parade held in peacetime is the "show of force," the very same tactic which the ancient Romans employed to frighten weaker countries into submission. Of all the shows of force which have been staged since the Romans' time, probably the most spectacular was held in France in the year 1520.

King Henry VIII of England and King Francis I of France had made a date to meet and discuss a possible military alliance between their two nations. Each of the kings cannily decided that he could better dictate the terms of the alliance if he demonstrated that he really didn't *need* an ally. So each of them put on a show intended to impress the other with his might and wealth. Henry brought an army to France and camped at the town of Guines. Francis brought his army to the nearby town of Ardres. Then, on the appointed day, they and all their troops marched out to meet in a field between. So splendid and sumptuous were their parades that the meeting is still referred to, in even the most solemn history books, as "The Field of Cloth of Gold."

The English king rode out from Guines preceded by five hundred guardsmen, two thousand infantrymen, archers, cavalrymen, and trumpeters. Henry was dressed in scarlet, "ribbed with gold." His horse wore gold harness and draperies inlaid with colored bits of mosaic. Henry was followed by his courtiers and nobles, all dressed in "cloth of tissue" (the finest gauze), their horses armored in golden scales. The French king's parade was led by a hundred Swiss spearmen and a band playing on trumpets, flutes, oboes, and drums. Francis wore a blouse adorned with diamonds, rubies, emeralds, and pearls, and over it a cape of cloth of gold. The remainder of the two parades were all soldiers garbed in their dress uniforms, their freshly polished armor and weapons flashing to make the eyes squint.

When the two tremendous processions met, they halted face to face and there was a moment of silence. Then there was a clamorous fanfare from the trumpets of both armies' bands. The two kings dismounted, embraced, and entered a huge silk pavilion for their conference. This lasted for twenty days, during which much of the kings' time was spent at feasting together and watching their champion warriors joust, fence, and wrestle in tournaments. All of this festivity and showing-off accomplished very little, however. The French-English alliance was never made, and the conference is remembered more for its glitter and glamour than for any real contribution to history.

THE FIELD OF CLOTH OF GOLD, *in France, was the scene of one of the most memorable "show of force" parades, when King Edward VIII and King Francis I met there in 1520.*

(BROWN BROTHERS)

Show-of-force parades get especially forceful in times of world stress, when there seems real danger of a war in the offing. In 1907, when Japan was first becoming a power to be reckoned with, President Theodore Roosevelt decided to shake an armored fist in that direction to show that the United States would not tolerate any military aggression in the Pacific. He staged an ocean-going parade that eventually "marched" all the way around the world.

The Great White Fleet, as it was called, consisted of sixteen brand-new, white-hulled battleships with crews totalling twelve thousand men. At the time it sailed, it was the mightiest sea force ever set afloat. The fleet steamed out of Hampton Roads, Virginia, in December, 1907, and didn't get back to home port until more than a year later, in February, 1909. It had rounded South America, touched at many Pacific lands, and come home by way of the Indian Ocean, the Suez Canal, the Mediterranean, and the North Atlantic. Along the way, the fleet had been given triumphal receptions in most of the ports where it anchored. Even Japan—however unwillingly and insincerely—arranged a festive welcome for it.

Unfortunately, the Great White Fleet turned out, after all, to be no great show of America's might. When it steamed off in prideful splendor, other navies were already busy designing and building the new "dreadnaught class" of battleships—much bigger, much more heavily armed and armored. By the time the Great White Fleet was only halfway through its parade around the world, it was almost as outclassed and out-of-date as the "invincible" Spanish Armada of 1588.

THE GREAT WHITE FLEET *of American battleships steams into San Francisco Bay, during its historic 1907-09 "parade" around the world.*

(U. S. NAVAL HISTORICAL FOUNDATION)

THIS MILITARY PARADE *of scout cars on a Madrid boulevard has one untypical feature—there's an Army guard-dog riding on the hood of each vehicle.*

(EMBASSY OF SPAIN)

Nowadays, the show of force is a peacetime maneuver usually intended to *keep* the peace. It is not so much an open threat as a warning: "Don't tread on me." On these occasions, a nation parades its most imposing units of fighting men, its heaviest tanks, fastest and biggest war planes, wickedest-looking artillery, and any other frightening weapons that are not classified "secret."

The United States parades its military might in many big cities on Armed Forces Day (the third Saturday in May) and sometimes on other patriotic holidays. Russia and its satellite Communist countries hold their biggest military displays on May Day and on November 7 (the anniversary of the revolution in 1917 that brought Communism into power).

On these parade days, foreign diplomats and military observers anxiously flock to Moscow's Red Square and to Washington's Pennsylvania Avenue to see what awesome new weapons these two strongest nations may be unveiling. At the Moscow parade in November, 1965, for instance, foreign visitors got their first look at a new Russian missile which the Communist leaders claim can be sent into orbit and kept there in space, ready to drop onto any target on earth.

MAY DAY IN MOSCOW, *and the traditional military parade features mighty missiles mounted on self-propelled launchers. The sign in the background seems rather out of place; it calls on all Russians to "do great deeds" in helping to boost farm food production.*

(SOVFOTO)

The United States is generally not so gruff and boastful, preferring to keep its newest weapons under wraps until and unless they're actually needed in action. But it has happened that even when the military men wanted to brandish a brand-new weapon, they just couldn't. On one Armed Forces Day a few years ago, the U. S. Army was eager to show off its new atomic cannon in New York, but the city wouldn't allow it. The gun weighed eighty tons, and would have crumbled the paving on the streets.

Although soldiers, sailors, and airmen do most of their peacetime parading on patriotic holidays, their post commanders are often willing to lend a marching unit or a band to a nearby town for such non-military occasions as civic anniversaries, receptions for celebrities, even religious celebrations. It may seem a bit unfair to the troops, to order them to help observe civilians' holidays. But the commanders reason that it's good practice for the men. And the troops themselves don't grumble too much; a parade can be a welcome break in the sometimes boring routine of peacetime service.

The military contingent is usually the most thrilling part of a civilian parade, especially if it includes a brass band. The men are all precisely lined up, wearing trim uniforms and carrying impressive weapons, colorful flags, or gleaming band instruments. They march like one smooth-functioning machine—quite often, they're the *only* people in the parade who march in step. Of course, they're trained to it; parade drill is one of the first things a recruit learns in any of the services. And the military takes its parades very seriously. To make sure they're precise and perfect, every single movement of a marching man is done according to strict regulations. For example:

"Marching personnel should not hunch, lean or stiffen, but should carry themselves erect and relaxed, with their head up and their chest out. Each man should step out smartly with a thirty-inch step. Swing your arms six inches to the front and three to the rear in a military manner."

Even the parader's eyes must remain fixed straight ahead in a "military manner." According to regulations, he cannot look sideways except on command. He must instantly respond to any order he hears, and if

A MOUNTED MILITARY PARADE *of Algerian* spahis *(cavalrymen), formerly French colonial troops, rides through Paris during a Bastille Day celebration.*
(FRENCH EMBASSY)

that command is "forward march!" he must go on marching straight ahead until he hears an order to halt or turn. Should his leader fail to shout such a command at the proper time, the soldier is expected to plod mechanically right along, even if it means that half the parade marches into a ditch or onto some startled family's front porch. (These and even funnier things have happened, when a parade commander got confused.)

American military men march more briskly than those in some other countries' services. The U. S. Army's marching standard is 120 steps per minute, while the French Foreign Legion, for instance, marches at a comparatively leisurely 78 steps per minute. There are shifts of speed—"double time!" and "half time!" to close up gaps in a parade or to space it out—and "mark time!" to keep the troops in step when the parade comes to a temporary halt. If a parade has to cross a bridge, you'll hear its commander order "route step!"—meaning for the men to get out of step and merely walk across, still in formation but at random pace. This is necessary because the vibration of all those simultaneous footsteps, if they marched in unison, would make the bridge shake and *could* even make it fall apart.

"EYES RIGHT!" *is the command, and every man of these marching Scots Guards —except the marcher in each right-side file—swivels his head to face the reviewing stand as he paces by.*

(BRITISH TRAVEL ASSOCIATION)

THE FIJI MILITARY BAND *in a marching and concert performance. The bandsmen up front are playing a unique sort of "drum"—pounding bamboo sticks on the arena ground.*

(COLUMBIA FESTIVALS, INC.)

Various military outfits are so proud of their marching ability and so fond of parades that, in peacetime at least, parading is their chief occupation. The British Army has several outfits which tour the world staging exhibition parades (for paying audiences, in arenas like New York's Madison Square Garden). Among these are the fantastically precise Marching Bands of the Royal Marines; the ever-popular, kilted troops of Scots Greys and Scots Guards, who march to the bagpipe and drum; and the even more colorful Fiji Military Band of spear-carrying native Fijian soldiers, whose uniforms include fringed skirts and bare feet, and whose band instruments include tom-toms and bamboo sticks for whacking on the ground.

The U. S. Army likewise has its exhibition marching units. One of the most distinctive is the Fife and Drum Corps of the 1st Battalion, 3rd Infantry. This outfit is stationed in Washington, D.C., but spends much of its time touring American and European cities. When on parade, the twenty-nine men of the corps wear authentic Continental Army uniforms of the Revolutionary War—black tricorn hats, white wigs, red greatcoats, brass-buckled shoes, white knee-breeches and stockings. They play on wooden fifes, antique bugles, and handmade drums which imitate those of Washington's time (the drumheads held taut by a zigzag of ropes). The drum major leads the band with a spontoon, a sort of combination battle-ax and spear that's taller than he is.

The service units taking part in a parade, whether a civilian or an all-military parade, must hold to a rigid order of precedence. That is, they follow a long-established tradition as to which service groups rightfully march in front of which others. The order of precedence is mainly based on the age of the services; for example, the United States

THE "OLD GUARD" *Fife and Drum Corps of the U.S. 3rd Infantry's 1st Battalion marches in a Washington parade. The drum major leads the corps with an eight-foot antique spontoon.*

(U.S. ARMY)

had an organized Army before it had a Navy (though only about two months before). So if a parade includes one unit of soldiers and one of sailors, the soldiers will march ahead of the sailors. If an American parade included units from *all* the various services, they would march in this order:

Up front, the cadets of the U. S. Military Academy (West Point).
Then, the midshipmen of the U. S. Naval Academy (Annapolis).
The cadets of the U. S. Air Force Academy.
The U. S. Army.
The U. S. Marine Corps.
The U. S. Navy.
The U. S. Air Force.
The U. S. Coast Guard.
The U. S. National Guard.
The Organized Reserve Corps (Army).
The Marine Corps Reserve.
The Naval Reserve.
The Air Force National Guard.
The Air Force Reserve.
And finally, the Coast Guard Reserve.

Warriors had been parading for countless thousands of years—first on foot, then on horseback, camelback, elephantback, on water and on wheels—before the twentieth century added a new dimension to parades. Now they're not only long and broad, they're high.

A big military parade doesn't seem really well-armed, these days, without at least one "flyover" of sleek, swift airplanes. The first sky paraders took part in the triumphal processions at the close of World War I. When the primitive war planes of that time flew over, they didn't move a *great* deal faster than the tanks and trucks on the ground. Nowadays, the jet planes zip along a parade's route so quickly that they may have to repeat their flyover several times, to make sure all the spectators catch a glimpse of them. They've added new sounds to parades, too—the sizzling screech of the whip-fast fighters, the rumbling thunder of the massive bombers, and sometimes, when the planes fling themselves through the sound barrier, the earth-jolting smack of the "sonic boom."

AIRPOWER ON PARADE. *This was a mighty air armada in its day—1936. These two-engined, open-cockpit, fixed-gear, biplane bombers lumbered along at a top speed of about 140 miles per hour.*

(U.S. AIR FORCE)

Most of the military sky parades are sternly businesslike, but there are sky clowns, too. Both the U. S. Air Force and the U. S. Navy have "aerobatic teams" of jet pilots who specialize in daredevil stunts. On parade occasions, they put their planes through tortuous maneuvers at screaming speed. They loop, bank, dive, roll, zoom straight up—either taking turns, one after another, or flying in formations so tight that their wingtips nearly touch. They are thrilling to watch—and hair-raisingly scary, too, but no spectator has ever been known to tear his eyes off them.

THE "THUNDERBIRDS," *the U.S. Air Force's aerobatic daredevils, who often participate in "flyover" parades, roar down the back arc of a loop in tight formation at speeds of better than 500 miles per hour.*

(U.S. AIR FORCE)

VII

"Here Come the Elephants!"

IT COULD BE SAID THAT the first circus parade ever held was the procession of animals that marched two by two into Noah's Ark to ride out the Flood. But we have better historical evidence for a water-borne parade that took place in ancient Egypt. About 1400 B.C., five boats sailed up the Nile River into the interior of Africa. They carried cargoes of spices to the land of Punt, and there traded them for a menagerie of assorted animals. When the boats sailed home again, the Egyptians living along the river were treated to quite a circus parade. They had never before seen such animals as rode the boats' decks: giraffes, monkeys, water buffalo, greyhounds, and other exotic creatures from the unknown lands.

Egypt kept on collecting animals from all over Africa until, shortly before the Christian era began, the city of Alexandria had a one hundred acre zoo. But the animals didn't just stand around to be looked at. They were continually being borrowed by the local princes and priests, to march or be carried in triumphal and religious processions.

One such parade, described by the Egyptian historian Atheneum, included two dozen elephants (each wearing golden draperies and an ivy-leaf crown), a dozen lions, sixty-six goats, fifteen water buffaloes, four wild asses, eight ostriches (pulling little carriages), seven stags, hundreds of sheep, and one Ethiopian rhinoceros. In addition, men marching in the procession carried branches to which were attached hundreds of beautiful birds and small animals like monkeys, civet cats, and lemurs. And last, but hardly least, the parade included *two thousand* sacred bulls.

The ancient Egyptians were also the first people to enjoy some other entertainments which were later to become part of the circus tradition. These were traveling shows of musicians, drummers, and dancers who wandered from one village to another, giving a street performance and then "passing the hat" for contributions from the onlookers.

Greek visitors to Egypt saw and liked these shows, and carried the idea back to their own land. There the traveling troupes (called *agyrtes*) added animals to their shows. The fiercer beasts were shown in cages; the tamer ones were trained to earn their keep by doing tricks. For example, the *agyrtes* were the first European shows to exhibit dancing bears.

The traveling entertainers and menageries next moved on to Rome, where the showmen were called *circulatores*. Several of these troupes displayed hippopotamuses; and after Roman times, oddly enough, no hippopotamus was ever exhibited in Europe again for nearly eighteen centuries. It wasn't until 1850 that one was sent from Egypt to the London Zoo. The Romans were also the first Europeans to see an elephant. In the third century B.C., the consul Metellus, warring against the Carthaginians in Africa, captured 142 of the elephants they used for pack animals, and brought them home to Rome. But this turned out to be a rather sad episode. After everyone in Rome had had a look at the beasts, nobody seemed to know what to do with them next. So they stampeded the whole herd off a cliff into the sea.

HERE COME THE ELEPHANTS— *as much a crowd-pleaser today as they were in the third century* B.C., *when Roman parade-watchers were the first Europeans to lay eyes on the mighty beasts.*

(OLD MILWAUKEE DAYS)

Meanwhile, Rome was inventing some other bits of show business that would eventually become part of the circus. Rome also gave us the word "circus" itself. Ordinarily the word meant simply "circle," but the Romans gave the name to a circular race track, and then to any sort of arena where exhibitions or contests were held. The Circus Maximus (or "greatest arena") was the scene of some spectacular shows. Though later circuses copied the idea of "spectacles," they had to tame them down considerably from what the Romans considered entertaining.

There were the *naumachia,* for instance, "sea battles" held on an artificial lake built inside the Circus Maximus. Model ships, smaller than real ones, were propelled by oarsmen while warriors on deck did the fighting. As many as six thousand men would be involved in a single one of these contests. And the battles were not always pretend-fights. Sometimes the warriors would be enacted by criminals who were let out of prison for the occasion and provided with real death-dealing weapons. Any who lived through the gory performance would be pardoned and freed. In another sort of show, an artificial whale "swam" across the Circus to where fifty gladiators were waiting, opened its mouth and disgorged fifty live bears to fight the gladiators to the death.

Every new show in the Circus Maximus was preceded by a parade called the *pompa circensis.* Led by the Roman nobles who would occupy the best seats at the performance, it usually marched to the Circus from the Forum (the center of the city). Behind the nobles marched the gladiators who would be part of the entertainment. Then came the horse-drawn cages of all the wild beasts that would fight and be fought. In a later era, when Rome was trying to stamp out Christianity, the parade also included the miserable Christian prisoners destined to be thrown, unarmed and helpless, before hungry lions and bears.

The extravagant Circus Maximus type of performance, and the parades that went with it, came to an end when the Roman Empire collapsed. But the other kind of show—the traveling troupes and menageries—continued to wander about Europe. Such a show might consist of just a single flute player and his dancing bear, or a group of jugglers, tumblers, musicians, and tightrope walkers. These little troupes couldn't manage much of a parade, beyond marching into town in a bunch, beating on drums and tambourines. But sometimes, when they played a large city, the tightrope walker would hurry there in advance, and be ready to walk a rope stretched between two rooftops high above the spectators' heads, while the rest of the show paraded along the street beneath.

By the eighteenth century, various European cities had revived the arena type of show, though not on such a scale as the Romans'. Phillip

Astley's show in London is regarded by most historians as being the first of the modern circuses. It starred Astley, his wife and little boy, who were all trick horseback riders; but it also presented tumblers, jugglers, rope-walkers, "human pyramids" of acrobats, and even one clown (known to history only as Burt). Other English circuses of the 1700's added the "sideshow" of freaks and oddities, such as "O'Brien the Irish Giant," who stood nine feet tall, and the first famous fat man, Edward Bright, who weighed 621¼ pounds.

The first showman to take his circus on the road was Thomas Taplin Cooke, in England in the early 1800's. This was a family affair; the troupe consisted of Cooke and his wife, their nineteen children, *their* wives, husbands, and children, sundry in-laws and other relations. From time to time, one of the younger Cookes would start a new show of his own. By the middle of that century, the various Cooke circuses were showing all over Europe.

Although the history of these early circuses is a fascinating subject, there is still no mention of organized parades—except for a march around the ring before every show. In those days of slow horse-transportation and poor roads, it was trouble enough just to get from one town to another, without trying to make a splendid production of it. Besides, the earliest road shows had so little to display that they

THIS "MUD SHOW"—*as a pokey little traveling circus is called—probably resembles the earliest circuses that went on the road in England in the early 1800's. This one is parading through North Yakima, Washington, in 1898.*
(CIRCUS WORLD MUSEUM)

really couldn't afford to show it off free in a parade. For example, there was a man named Hachaliah Bailey, who toured the eastern United States about 1815, showing off his one elephant (named Old Bet) in farm barns and tavern yards. To keep people from getting a look at Old Bet without paying, Bailey had to lead her from place to place in the dead of night. Any midnight travelers who did get a free look were probably frightened out of a year's growth when that house-sized monster suddenly loomed out of the darkness.

Many later menageries, too, had to march by night, but for another reason. Nineteenth-century America was extremely religious, and there were many people—especially in the backward country areas—who thought Sunday entertainment was a sin, and who hated the traveling circuses because they wouldn't close on Sundays. Such people would often grab up a gun and shoot to kill the "sinful" menagerie animals as they passed. Obviously, in those times and in those areas, parades were out of the question. (Though the showmen tried to make their circuses sound suitable for Sunday by giving them names like "A Modern Noah's Ark" and "Animals of the Scriptures.")

Fortunately, the civilized city folk were more tolerant of entertainers. And so it was in the city of Albany, New York, that the very first modern-day circus parade was held, on a May day in 1837. Unlike other circus owners, Purdy, Welch, Macomber and Company had decided that a small preview of their show's delights might well tempt people to want to pay to see the rest of it. The parade was indeed only a *small* preview; it consisted merely of some trumpeters on horseback and a few drummers riding on elephants. But it worked. The people of Albany crowded the main street to watch the little procession pass, and then followed it to the circus grounds, ticket money in hand.

"A STREAM OF GOLD AND GLITTER," *the circus parade was called in the 1890's. While this one, marching into Decatur, Illinois, doesn't exactly merit such extravagant comment, it was evidently spectacular enough to draw an admiring crowd.*
(CIRCUS WORLD MUSEUM)

Showmen everywhere soon realized that a parade was the best advertisement a circus could have, and within another twenty years the circus parade was entering its Golden Age. By the 1850's the parades had grown to include brass bands with the elegantly-uniformed players riding atop special bandwagons, wild animals in special cage-wagons, cavorting clowns, strange music-making machines, rank after rank of horsemen (and women), herds of elephants and camels. Amongst them marched every other member of the troupe, from star performers to the elephants' water-boy, most of these in gaudy, spangled costumes. The circus parade had become what a newspaper of the time described as "a stream of gold and glitter, a mile long."

The parades' wagons were something to behold. The cage-wagons had their sides carved or painted with animal scenes from the Bible— Daniel in the lion's den, Jonah and the whale, and others. The cage-wagons for hippopotamuses, seals, and polar bears had built-in wading pools. Those for the large and clumsy beasts, like the hippo, were often

A GAUDY AND GILDED WAGON, *once the pride of the Pawnee Bill Wild West Show, bears a hand-carved depiction of the Indian princess Pocahontas saving Captain John Smith from death on the headsman's chopping block.*
(OLD MILWAUKEE DAYS)

THIS OLD-TIME HIPPO WAGON *was built with a bulging "bay window" on each side so the hippopotamus could turn around comfortably.*

(OLD MILWAUKEE DAYS)

constructed with a bulging "bay window" on either side, to make room for the animal to turn around comfortably.

The tableau wagons were similar to today's floats, carrying carved scenes from mythology, fairy tales, and Mother Goose. Some wagons were covered all over with expensive gold leaf instead of mere paint. Others bore plate-glass mirrors finer than those in the richest homes. The Robinson circus had one wagon in the shape of a huge peacock. The Sells-Floto circus's ticket-office wagon was built in the shape of a little cottage. Several circuses owned "telescope" wagons that weighed ten tons or more, and displayed five or six different tableaus on different levels. These wagons shut up like a telescope for traveling convenience. At parade time, men cranked windlasses that opened them up to the height of a three-storey building.

Such wagons were, of course, far too valuable to be used for hauling anything, except at parade time. While traveling between shows they wore plush-lined protective covers of wood or canvas, and sometimes were carried inside wagons of their own. A single one of their ornately-carved "sunburst" wheels cost as much as $150 to make. The Barnum and Bailey circus had a bandwagon known as the "Two Hemispheres" because it bore the carved, gilded coats-of-arms of countries of both the Old and the New World. It cost $40,000 to build, and would cost at least $200,000 to copy today. Many of the circus wagons were built and carved by the same artisans who made the ships' figureheads and cigar-store wooden Indians of that era. But the very best wagons came from carvers in Italy (who had formerly specialized in making statues of

ANTIQUE CIRCUS WAGONS, *awaiting the start of the 1965 "Old Milwau-kee Days" parade, include (in the foreground) tableau wagons depict-ing the Old Woman Who Lived in a Shoe and Cinderella and her prince.*
(OLD MILWAUKEE DAYS)

saints for churches). Some American circuses imported the Italian-made wagons; others sent for the carvers themselves to come to America.

The wagons' teams were often as eye-filling as the wagons they pulled. The Sells Brothers circus, for example, had one team of ten horses, five black, five white, who were always hitched up in twos—alternately black-white and white-black, "checkerboard fashion." Some-times a team would step out proudly in a harness made of gleaming white patent leather with silver-plated trimmings.

Barnum and Bailey's "Two Hemispheres" wagon was so heavy that it required a team of *forty* horses to pull it and three men to drive it. One man's job was just to tend to the wheel brakes; another was constantly busy keeping the reins straight. The chief driver had to be a man of considerable strength and skill, because he really had his hands full, holding (and controlling) ten reins in each fist. The forty horses were hitched up four abreast; the lead horses were eighty feet ahead of the wagon. When the team turned a corner, twenty feet of the outside reins had to slip through the driver's fingers, and then be gathered in again as the team straightened out.

Circus people early realized that even the biggest band of musicians can sometimes sound puny in the open air. So they invented some fantastic machines for making louder parade music. One of the first was the Spalding and Rogers circus's "Apollonicon," which contained organ pipes, whistles, horns, drums, triangles, gongs, and cymbals. The Apollonicon's inventor, Henry Green, claimed that it could produce "the music of one thousand instruments."

The Yankee Robinson circus had the "Polyhymnia," a fifteen-foot-high pipe organ on wheels. P. T. Barnum's first circus had a monstrosity that was screechingly loud, if not exactly musical, called the "Devil's Whistle." The Ringling Brothers circus had a bellwagon, containing eight immense bells played by a piano-like keyboard. Although the contraption had been built in America, the circus called it "The Grand Russian Cathedral Chimes." According to the parade posters, this music-maker rang out in "deep, rolling, heaving, changing, swelling, sinking, rising, overwhelming, exalting peals . . ."

But the widest-used, best-loved and longest-lasting of all such inventions was the calliope, created by Josh Stoddard in 1855. The Greek name means "beautiful voice," and is correctly pronounced "cal-LYE-o-pee," but circus folk have always called it "cally-ope." It is essentially a set of giant whistles blown by steam pressure, which means that the calliope wagon must carry a water boiler and a heater of some sort. On the older models this was a wood or coal stove that had to be continuously stoked by an assistant. The man who played the calliope's piano-type keyboard—he was always dignified with the title of "professor"—required strong fingers, because each of the keys had to open a valve that was held closed by 120 pounds of steam pressure. (Some later calliopes were powered by tanks of compressed air, but real circus fans wouldn't call *them* calliopes at all.)

THE APOLLONICON COMES TO TOWN. *This rather exaggerated nineteenth-century drawing shows a 40-horse team hauling the musical machine called the Apollonicon (shown here much larger than it really was).*

(N.Y. PUBLIC LIBRARY)

A TROOP OF SMALL BOYS, *awed and admiring, trails along beside a steam calliope as it brings up the rear of a 1908 circus parade. Dimly visible inside the wagon is the "professor" who played the contraption.*

(CIRCUS WORLD MUSEUM)

One of the endearing things about the calliope was that it was so often hilariously out of tune. The pitch of each whistle would change if the steam pressure rose or fell, and it was practically impossible to keep the pressure at a constant 120 pounds. But even if the tune the professor played was usually full of false notes, the steam-blasted low tones would rattle every window on a parade street, and the shrill high notes could be heard a full five miles away.

The calliope had this drawback: its high-pressure boiler might blow up at any moment. It frequently did, giving the parade a brief but spectacular fountain display and giving the parade-watchers a hot bath. But the saddest thing about the calliope was that it almost always was the last wagon in the procession (so it wouldn't out-thunder the band-wagon up front). When the calliope came down the street, you knew the parade was over.

Besides the familiar sort of circus, there were other kinds touring America in the nineteenth century. There were the Wild West shows, one of which was led by the famous scout "Buffalo Bill" Cody. These shows featured trick riding, sharpshooting, mock-battles of Indians versus wagon trains and Indians versus the U. S. Cavalry. Their street parades included stagecoaches, ox-drawn covered wagons, cowboys and cowgirls, Indians and cavalrymen on horseback, a buffalo or two, and sometimes a few Roman chariots.

Gilbert Spalding and Charles Rogers, whose circus owned the Apollonicon music machine, moved their troupe from the land to the water,

REAL LIVE INDIANS, *troupers in a Wild West circus, are shown in this old photograph awaiting the form-up of the day's parade.*

(N.Y. PUBLIC LIBRARY)

and thereby invented the showboat. Theirs might better have been called a show *fleet,* because it consisted of a whole parade of boats that entertained up and down the Ohio and Mississippi rivers throughout the 1850's. Leading the parade came a tugboat bearing the Apollonicon, whose weird music echoed for miles through the river valleys, to bring people scurrying to the riverside. Behind the tug came two flatboats carrying the Spalding and Rogers menagerie. Finally came the circus proper on a tremendous barge, the "Floating Palace," big enough to stage a one-ring show and seat more than two thousand spectators.

But in the heyday of the traveling show, the "regular" circus was by far the most common and numerous. There were so many of them that they often had to compete—not always politely—for the same piece of territory. And when two circuses found themselves playing the same town on the same day, as sometimes happened, trouble was sure to break out. Each circus would hustle to get its parade on the streets first, but they'd both get there eventually, and for a while the townspeople would enjoy a double helping of entertainment. But inevitably the two parades would tangle, jam up in confusion, and then dissolve into a free-for-all fight with fists and tent stakes. On at least one occasion, the brawlers overturned several cage-wagons and let loose a number of wild animals who enthusiastically joined the fight. That, the townspeople did not enjoy.

Circus parades have had other misadventures. Many years ago, in one parade, a small baby elephant rode all by himself atop a high tableau wagon. A young circus worker was supposed to be keeping an eye on him, but didn't notice that the elephant was reaching up with his trunk to snatch a mouthful of leaves off each tree he passed. At one point, the little fellow got a trunkhold on a branch that refused to break. The wagon kept going, out from under him, and the crowd was astonished and amused to see an elephant dangling high in midair. After a moment the branch snapped and dropped him into the street. The baby elephant wasn't hurt at all, but his young keeper was so shaken by the incident that he quit show business on the spot, and was last seen heading homeward to his family farm.

A circus did not actually parade from one town to the next. It did its between-town traveling at night, either in its own horse-drawn wagons or, as many shows did in the late 1800's, with its wagons lined up on railroad flatcars. It arrived at the circus grounds (usually a meadow outside town) sometime before dawn, while the townspeople were still abed. The first job was to get the big tents erected and everything ready for the day's business. Then the troupers changed from overalls into costumes, and started forming up the parade.

The special decorated wagons were taken out of their protective covers. The ordinary traveling wagons that had brought the circus—even the cook-wagon and the dressing-room wagons—were dressed up with ribbons, bunting, and banners to make them look like something fancier than mere transportation. Everything and everybody that took part in the procession had to be as bright, gaudy, and circus-y as possible. Even the wagon-drivers, who usually wore no special garb, were instructed *not* to parade in shirt-sleeves or with their vests unbuttoned, and *not* to smoke or chew tobacco or spit while they were on display.

By the time all the horses were hitched up, and the elephants were all in line (trunk to tail to trunk), and the bandsmen had all blown the early morning dew out of their tubas and sousaphones, the town would be up and doing, and ready for the parade. No doubt the schools would be closed for the occasion—as much for the teachers' benefit as the children's. It is recorded that in one Montana town even the Criminal Court adjourned, and the judge, jury, bailiffs, and accused prisoner all attended the parade together.

Before the parade could march into town, the "fixers" had to be sent in ahead. These were circus workmen who weren't needed in the procession. They stood along the parade route to bellow the warning, "Hold yer hosses! Here come the elephants!" (Horses hate the smell of elephants, and are inclined to stampede.) The fixers also carried a

pocketful of free circus passes to hand out to anybody whose horses did bolt, or to pacify anybody else who was annoyed by the parade. They also had to keep an eye on the kids in the crowd, who might toss firecrackers under the elephants' bellies.

Sometimes the parade had to wait while the town lined up a marching contribution of its own—perhaps a platoon of dome-helmeted policemen, or the new steam fire engine it was so proud of. If any towns-people owned automobiles, these would likely be invited to join the procession, too; cars were almost as much of a curiosity in the 1890's as giraffes were. Sometimes the town's mayor himself joined the parade, strutting and bowing beside the whip-cracking ringmaster.

Eventually everything was ready. The crowd of people along the sidewalks held their breath and craned to peer up the street. There was a short hush, then a blare of music. And the parade marched in.

No word description of an oldtime circus parade can really tell you what it was like. Even pictures that show what it looked like can't capture the excitement of the occasion. And neither words nor pictures can convey the sounds of it: the thump, crash, and oompah of the brass band; the oohs and aahs of the crowd; the tramp of marching feet and clop-clop of hooves; the clanking of the wagons' chains; the creak and jingle of harness; the street-quaking rumble of the massive iron-rimmed wheels; the heavy, leathery scuff of the elephants' great feet; the flop-flop pad-along of the camels; the unearthly, jolly-mournful wail of the steam calliope; the hair-raising roar of a lion (if you were lucky) just as his cage passed in front of you . . .

And the smells! Some of them were familiar—perhaps not now, but then—the smells of saddle soap, axle grease, brass polish, new paint, horse droppings, dusty street underfoot and green trees overhead. Some of the smells were less common: the nose-wrinkling sharpness of gunpowder smoke from exploding firecrackers; the scent of cedar sawdust and shredded oak bark that lined the cages' bottoms; perhaps a whiff of real perfume from a lady bareback rider. And some of the smells you *never* smelled until the circus came to town. Try to imagine the odor of an old leather suitcase stuffed full of sweet hay: that was the elephants. A heavy, musky, jungle-warm smell: that was the lions and tigers. The damp green smell of a mossy riverbank: that was the

YESTERYEAR, *the circus parade was a common summer sight in almost every American community. But when this picture was taken in 1925, the fast-multiplying automobile was already beginning to crowd the parade off the streets.*

(CIRCUS WORLD MUSEUM)

hippo in his tank-wagon. The blended smells of coal smoke, laundry steam, and hot metal: that was the calliope. And there were hints of other circus smells—perhaps you only imagined them, or looked forward to them—popcorn, cotton candy, hot dogs, sliced watermelon, ice cream cones, candied apples-on-a-stick, pink lemonade . . .

Of all the circus parades ever held, the gaudiest were those staged by Phineas T. Barnum, history's most famous showman. Barnum is so well remembered as the man who made the circus "the greatest show on earth" that most people are surprised to learn that he never had anything to do with a circus until he was sixty years old. By that time, he had already made his fame and fortune as a showman, with his American Museum, a New York theater of freaks and oddities. But in 1871 he bought a share in a small circus, gave it his name and began to make it grow. Barnum's was the first two-ring, and then the first three-ring, circus in America. When he joined forces with his foremost competitor, James A. Bailey, the combined Barnum and Bailey circus was the biggest on the planet.

To celebrate their merger, Barnum and Bailey staged a parade in New York City on Saturday night, March 26, 1881. A newspaper called it "the grandest pageant ever witnessed in our streets." Barnum talked the city into stringing cables along the parade streets to illuminate the show with that new invention: electric lights. (*"The Avenues Ablaze with Prismatic Hues!"* proclaimed the advertisements.) Spectators paid apartment-dwellers along the route as much as $10.00 apiece for a seat at their windows, and a dollar in those days was worth five of today's.

"A Veritable Cyclone of Wonders and Tornado of Magnificent Objects!" Barnum's advertisements promised. *"Bewildering Array of Costly Novelties, and a very Vesuvius of Brilliant Features! The Mightiest and, Absolutely, the Perfection of All Great Public Processions!"* And everyone agreed that the parade lived up to its publicity. It was on the streets for more than four hours. It included 370 of the circus's men and women performers, 338 horses, a score of elephants, and hundreds of other animals, both caged and afoot. The wild-animal trainers actually rode inside the cages of their lions, tigers, and leopards, and put them through their tricks while the parade was in motion.

"The golden chariots, triumphal and tableau cars," said the next day's newspapers, "were more numerous, more ponderous, more elaborate and gorgeous in finish than any other establishment has brought here." In addition to those drawn by teams of matched horses, there were wagons hitched to elephants, camels, zebras, elks—and miniature wagons drawn by ponies. The troops of horsemen were dressed in the uniforms of "the cavalry of all nations." The parade's music was furnished by a calliope, a bellwagon, a mobile pipe organ, a squad of Scottish bagpipers, a choral wagon carrying a company of Negro "plantation jubilee singers," and a total of four brass bands, one of them composed entirely of Indians in tribal costumes.

Barnum brought the circus to its peak; after his time it began to slip downhill. There just weren't any more showmen as flamboyant as Barnum to capture the public's imagination. And other entertainments— stage plays, vaudeville, even opera companies—began to venture into the smaller cities and towns. After the turn of the twentieth century came the movies, and then radio, to give the circuses still more competition. Gradually the smaller shows folded their tents, and the medium-sized ones merged with a handful of big ones. But even the biggest circuses became reluctant to stage a street parade, because American towns were fast filling up with automobiles. A parade could paralyze traffic for half a day, and make more enemies than friends. From the 1920's on, the parades were short and seldom. America's very last, real, oldtime circus parade marched in 1939.

But in recent years, to the great delight of circus fans, one such parade has been revived. It is something of an oddity: a circus parade without a circus.

The city of Milwaukee, Wisconsin, every year around the fourth of July, holds a city-wide festival called Old Milwaukee Days. In 1963, the Schlitz Brewing Company enlivened the holiday by sponsoring an old-fashioned circus parade, and has repeated it each summer since. The parade has attracted so much publicity and praise—and so many visitors from all over the continent—that it seems sure to continue as an annual tradition.

The equipment for the parade is provided by the Circus World Mu-

TODAY, *America enjoys just one circus parade a year, and it isn't even part of a circus. This is the yearly parade sponsored by the Schlitz Brewing Company as part of the "Old Milwaukee Days" celebration in that Wisconsin city.*

(OLD MILWAUKEE DAYS)

seum of Baraboo, Wisconsin, and the procession is organized and directed by the museum's curator, C. P. ("Chappie") Fox. The museum owns the world's largest collection of old circus wagons, some of them seventy years old but now refurbished like new. They were once the pride and joy of such long-gone circuses as the Gollmar Brothers', Al G. Barnes', the Pawnee Bill Wild West Show, and the P. J. Spellman "U. S. Motorized Circus." Many of the costumes and uniforms for the Milwaukee parade are created by the Circus World Museum's wardrobe mistress (and former trapeze artist), Mrs. Mayme Ward.

The wagons are transported from the Baraboo museum to Milwaukee on a long railroad train of flatcars, drawn by an antique steam locomotive. During the 125-mile haul, the train pauses at depots along the way to serenade the local folk with a concert on the steam calliope. In Milwaukee, at parade time, the wagons are hitched up to matched teams of handsome draft horses—purebred Percherons, Belgians, and Clydesdales. The horses are lent by ranchers and farmers from as far away as New York State and Ontario, Canada.

For the 1965 parade, Milwaukee mustered forty wagons, more than three hundred horses, twenty-three bands—and, for good measure, fifty antique automobiles. The Ringling Brothers and Barnum & Bailey Circus lent a score of elephants and a variety of wild animals to ride in the old cage-wagons. Some 600,000 people crowded the city's sidewalks to watch the procession—almost every soul in Milwaukee, plus tourists, circus fans, and news reporters from all over the United States.

The Milwaukee parade is a beautiful re-creation—actually longer than any that even the mighty Barnum ever put together—and well worth traveling to see. All it lacks is a real tent circus waiting in some sunlit meadow outside town, for the folks to flock to, after the old calliope has tootled away into the distance and the parade is over.

THE CAGE WAGON, *part of the "Old Milwaukee Days" parade, is seventy years old. The tigers are considerably younger. They were lent by a real circus to ride in the 1965 parade.*

(OLD MILWAUKEE DAYS)

"cornet," and the name of "tuba" is now given to a large, bass-voiced instrument used mainly in military and circus bands. The Romans also had a kind of trumpet called a *buccina*, and that word was gradually changed into our "bugle."

In the year A.D. 284, the legions put on a mass marching exhibition in Rome. It was probably a splendid spectacle; it was most certainly a noisy one. The troops marched to the music of a three-hundred-man band: one hundred *tuba* players, one hundred flute players and one hundred *cornu* players. But the Roman armies used their musical instruments for more than just entertainment. They learned that, even in the confused and clamorous midst of battle, the boom of a drum or the blare of a horn could be heard—and could be used by a commander to direct the actions of his separate units. Thus guided by musical signals, the Roman legions coolly and efficiently demolished the armies of enemies who had never thought of such a thing.

But in time the Roman Empire fell apart. And everything that the Romans had learned about military and parade music (and had taught to the rest of Europe), all that was soon forgotten. Indeed, music of any and every sort became scarce in Europe for the next six hundred years or so—the period known to historians as the Dark Ages. What silenced music for so long was the coming of Christianity.

The older religions of Europe had used music liberally in their ceremonies and parades. Now, since the newly-converted Christians scorned the old religions, they also rejected everything connected with them—including their music and musical instruments. So all but a few forms of music were forbidden to be heard. The Christians allowed the playing of the *syrinx* (better known as the "pipes of Pan") because it was associated with the Bible story of David as a shepherd boy, and they allowed the various plucked-string instruments, because David had played *them* when he was older and a composer of psalms. They also allowed the trumpet, because the Bible said that instrument would sometime sound the announcement of Judgment Day. But everything else was silenced—flutes, fifes and other woodwinds, drums, gongs, cymbals, and all the reed instruments.

Happily, outside of Europe music continued to develop. Its use as a military tool was especially kept up in the Moslem countries of the Near East. The Saracens never went into battle without a band of drums, trumpets, and shawms (an early woodwind instrument that later became the oboe and bassoon). They had learned that the music stimulated their own troops, who were accustomed to it, and struck terror into others, who weren't. The band served another purpose, too. In those times, an army always aimed its attack at the enemy's battle flag, because that marked his command post, the "heart" of his operations. So, on the battlefield, the Saracens grouped their musicians around the foot of their flagstaff. As long as the Saracen warriors could hear the band still playing, they knew that their flag still stood.

Europe came into contact with this Eastern music when the first Crusaders marched against the Saracens. As we have seen, these knights brought home with them what they'd learned from the enemy about military music. They also brought home samples of the Eastern instruments—shawms, mandolins, all kinds of drums, lutes, and rebecs (ancestors of the violin). These novelties helped bring about a rebirth of music in Europe, particularly as an accompaniment to parades.

In later centuries, other European travelers to the Near East were impressed by the parade music of the Turkish Janizaries (the sultan's royal guardsmen). As one visiting musician remarked, "The character of this music is so warlike that even cowardly souls take courage." What made it so inspiringly warlike, he said, was that "the first beat of each bar is so strongly marked with a new and manly accent that it is virtually impossible to get out of step." This was really no new thing— people had simply forgotten that the Roman legions once marched to the same sort of music. But now the European bandsmen gladly borrowed the Janizaries' practice of putting a heavy stress on the marching beat. And we still hear it today in the characteristic drum thump and deep bass oompah of parade music.

A BANDWAGON *designed for a triumphal parade honoring the sixteenth-century German Emperor Maximilian carries four men and a woman playing on the sackbut (left) and various-sized shawms.*

On one occasion or another, people have paraded to the music of just about every instrument that has ever been made—including such unwieldy oddities as the calliope and Apollonicon. But in general, paraders prefer instruments that meet two requirements: they must be easy to carry and they must make a noise loud enough to be appreciated in the open air.

The necessity for making them portable has had a lot to do with the shapes that some instruments wear today. The trumpet, for instance, was in its earliest form a very long, straight tube. But when trumpets were carried in a parade, the ranks of players had to march uncomfortably far apart in order not to clunk each other in the head when they raised the horns to their lips. So the Romans bent their trumpet (the *buccina*) into a wide circle, looping it up and backward over the player's shoulder. In the Middle Ages, trumpeters gave their instruments another kink, into an S shape. Through succeeding centuries, the trumpet continued to fold inward on itself, in tighter and tighter coils, until it acquired the complex but compact shape it has today. Various other wind instruments have done the same. The brass instrument called the French horn can easily be tucked under one arm, but if it were unkinked and stretched out straight it would be more than twelve feet long.

EARLY-DAY TRUMPETS, *as seen in this sixteenth-century engraving of a Venice parade, were long, straight pipes, so unwieldly that the bandsmen had to depend on young assistants to support them.*

(N.Y. PUBLIC LIBRARY)

SEI TROMBE | DI ARZENTO   SEX   TVBÆ ARGENTEÆ

Of all the instruments that have best combined loudness and portability, probably the loudest is the bagpipe. It not only makes plenty of noise, it can make it non-stop. The instrument has a leather bag which the player keeps full of air by blowing through a mouthpiece or, in some models, by pumping a small bellows under one arm. This stored-up air is then forced in a steady stream through the playing pipes by the pressure of the piper's elbow against the bag. He plays the melody by fingering the holes in a "chanter" pipe. Meanwhile, two or three "drone" pipes, each tuned to a single note, keep up a continuous wail of background noise.

The instrument is commonly regarded as a purely Scottish invention, but actually the bagpipe came to Scotland from Ireland. It has long been equally familiar to Spain, Portugal, Italy, France, and other countries as well. So far as can be determined, the bagpipe was invented by the ancient Phoenicians, and their far-wandering traders introduced it to all those other places.

AN ANCIENT WOODCUT *shows Irish brigands looting and burning a straw-thatched village. Notice that the marauders are marching to the music of a single bagpiper.*

JAUNTY AND COLORFUL *in kilts, plaids, and bearskin busbies, a troop of modern-day Scottish pipers parades along the London Embankment near Tower Bridge.*

(BRITISH TRAVEL ASSOCIATION)

When Scotland became part of Great Britain and contributed military units to the British Army, these brought along their bagpipers. A regimental bagpipe-and-drum band is led by a "pipe major" instead of a drum major, and, in certain Scottish regiments, the pipe major is the only enlisted soldier who is allowed to wear a beard. When the pipes bellow and screech a *pibroch* (a war march) they serve the same purpose as the Saracens' music did—stirring up the Scotsmen's fighting blood and paralyzing with fright the soldiers they march against. But even some of those armies they have frightened have later taken a liking to the bagpipes. And several of the countries which Britain once conquered and colonized—India and Afghanistan, for example—now have military bagpipe bands of their own.

There have been odder bands than those of bagpipes. In the eighteenth century, the Russian Army's most famous band consisted of thirty-five soldiers, each of whom carried a horn that could play just *one note*. The horns ranged in size from little soprano squeakers nine inches long to deep bass grunters twelve *feet* long. When the band played a tune, each man would sound his horn at just the precise instant his one note was called for in the score. Obviously this required a great deal of practicing beforehand, and a master conductor to lead the performance, but it is said that the band produced really well-meshed and melodious music.

However, in most of Europe from the fifteenth century onward, marching bands became rather standardized. The German infantry set the standard for other armies' foot soldiers; they marched to a band of flutes and snare drums. This eventually became the fife-and-drum band that is still traditional for the infantry to this day. The cavalry regiments, having more prestige than the infantry, were accompanied by the showier trumpets and kettledrums. Royal and noble personages, when they marched in procession—at coronations, for instance—usually stepped to the music of shawms and sackbuts (trumpets with telescoping slide-pipes, the ancestors of today's trombones).

The big brass band so familiar today wasn't born until after the French Revolution of the 1790's. That Revolution, in overthrowing the royal rule of France, aimed at winning liberty and equality for all Frenchmen. But it had lesser ambitions, too, and somewhere on the list was the aim of making good music available to the common man. Always before, the music of the concert hall had been the luxury of the rich and idle classes. But now, proclaimed the revolutionaries in 1793, "Our public squares will be our concert halls!"

A **MOUNTED BAND** *of the French Republican Army during post-Revolution days, playing bassoons, clarinets, horns, and trumpets. Notice that the near-side horn-player is muting his instrument by putting his fist inside the bell.*

And that's just about what happened. Even before the Revolution was over, Frenchmen were celebrating its victory at festivals in their town squares. Every citizen who could play a musical instrument would gather nightly in an improvised band to play stirring war songs and marches. Even serious composers wrote pieces for these concerts, to show that they were on the side of the common folk.

The people's concerts made it fashionable for military music to be played by large groups of many different instruments. So the first officially organized band of the new French Republican Army consisted of one flute, six clarinets, three bassoons, one trumpet, two French horns, one serpent, a bass drum, and a pair of cymbals. (That "serpent," by the way, wasn't a snake. It was an oldtime instrument on the order of a super-cornet, made of brass and wood, and curved in the shape of two S's stuck end to end. Even with all its snaky curves, it stood as tall as a man.)

From that time on, the tendency was for bands to get even larger and louder. It was for a military band that the great French composer, Hector Berlioz, wrote his vastest composition—the "Funereal and Triumphal Symphony," which called for more than two hundred brass and woodwind instruments. He wrote it in 1838 to accompany the ceremonial burial of French soldiers who had died while putting down a rebellion in the colony of Algeria. Berlioz himself, strutting in the uniform of a National Guardsman, conducted the gigantic band as the funeral paraded through the streets of Paris.

THESE BASS TUBAS, *the creation of nineteenth-century bandmaster Wilhelm Wiesprecht, are typical of the loud-but-portable kind of instruments developed especially for the marching band.*

(COLUMBIA FESTIVALS, INC.)

In that same year of 1838, in Berlin, sixteen infantry regiments and sixteen cavalry regiments of the Prussian Army massed all their separate bands into one, to play a triumphal reception march for the visiting Czar Nicholas I of Russia. All together, the thirty-two bands totalled one thousand wind instruments and two hundred drums. The stupendous job of conducting this musical army was undertaken by Prussia's chief bandmaster, Wilhelm Wiesprecht, who is otherwise memorable as the inventor of the brass horn called the bass tuba.

Besides Wiesprecht, several other nineteenth century musicians created new instruments—loud ones, easy to carry—with the intent of giving the parade band greater range and melodic capabilities. From France came Adolphus Sax's 1840 invention, the saxophone, now oftenest seen in jazz bands. The American bandmaster, John Philip Sousa, made a most distinctive contribution to the parade band when, in the 1890's, he took an oldtime instrument called the helicon and redesigned it into the big bass sousaphone. This is that tremendous brass horn that coils around a player's body, with its great flared bell peering over his shoulder (or even over his head, if he happens to be a short man). It is what puts the gruffest, growliest oompah into today's parade music.

In almost every parade that marches nowadays, at least one sousaphone goes swaggering and booming by. This is only right and proper, because there's scarcely a parade that doesn't march to the music that John Philip Sousa wrote. In his day (he died in 1932) he was known as "the March King." First as conductor of the U. S. Marine Band, and then leading his own band in performances all around the world, he composed for them more than one hundred colorful, rousing marches. He also wrote comic operas and other sorts of music, but, while these are long forgotten, his band compositions—"The Stars and Stripes Forever," "The Washington Post March," "The Liberty Bell," and a good many others—are still staunchly marching on.

Other composers, whom musicians consider far more "classical" then Sousa, have also written boom-crash-and-oompah march music. Berlioz has already been mentioned. The greatest composer of them all, Ludwig Beethoven, wrote a "Turkish March" into his music for an 1811 play, *The Ruins of Athens*. Giuseppe Verdi re-created an Egyptian parade with the "Triumphal March" in his 1871 opera, *Aïda*. In the opera's more lavish productions, real horses and elephants (sometimes even tame lions, ostriches, etc.) join the costumed Egyptian soldiers, priests, and nobles in parading onstage to this music.

At almost every church wedding today, the bride paces slowly down the aisle to the "Bridal Chorus" (commonly called "Here Comes the Bride") from Richard Wagner's 1850 opera, *Lohengrin*. And after the

THE BRASS BAND *is now universally popular. This one, marching through a Belgian town, has all the familiar instruments: trap drums, snare drums, bass drum, horns, and—towering over all—the bold, booming, big-belled sousaphones.*

(BELGIAN GOVT. INFORMATION CENTER)

ceremony, she and her new husband stride out of the church to the soaring "Wedding March" from the music which Felix Mendelssohn composed in 1826, inspired by Shakespeare's play, *A Midsummer Night's Dream*. Anyone who has ever attended a high school or college commencement ceremony has no doubt watched the graduates march in procession to the music of Sir Edward Elgar's 1901 "Pomp and Circumstance March."

In 1917, Erik Satie composed *Parade*, an entire ballet suite built around a circus procession. In Douglas Moore's 1924 orchestral suite, *The Pageant of P. T. Barnum*, he (quite naturally) included the music of a circus parade, and in it the steam calliope is imitated by the doleful bleating of a deliberately out-of-tune clarinet. Walter Piston's 1938 ballet, *The Incredible Flutist*, also contains a circus parade, and written into the musical score are the loud cheers, applause, and whistles of the sidewalk spectators. Two parade marches composed very recently have already taken their place among the all-time classics—Kenneth Alford's cheerful band arrangement of an old British folk tune, the "Colonel Bogey March" from the 1957 movie, *The Bridge on the River Kwai*; and the rollicking "Seventy-Six Trombones" from Meredith Willson's 1958 musical comedy, *The Music Man*.

Of all kinds of music, the march is the one most likely to set your foot tapping to the beat. But there are variations on the standard march rhythm. The military sometimes uses a quickstep march, more of a jogtrot than a walking step. There's the sedate wedding march; *Lohengrin*'s "Bridal Chorus" is a good example. And there's the even slower-paced funeral march—or the "dead march" as it is called by the military. Frédéric Chopin's *Marche Funèbre* is the oftenest heard.

And not all parades step to a march rhythm. You'll recall the Luxembourg procession of St. Willibrod's Day, when the paraders dance along to a polka tempo. In many other countries, the parades are accompanied by the local folk music. Nowadays, really roisterous parades—such as those held at Carnival time—often are accompanied by jazz bands. Though we think of jazz music as best suited to night clubs and indoor parties, it really has every right to perform in parades. That's where it made its first public appearances.

Jazz music was the creation of the American Negroes, based largely on what they remembered of their native African music. For a long time, it was played only at Negro gatherings, by "pick-up" bands of whatever players and instruments were on hand—most of the players self-taught and many of the instruments homemade. But in New Orleans, shortly before the turn of the twentieth century, it became the custom for a band to accompany Negro funeral processions to the graveyard. On the way to the burial, a band would play hymns and spirituals while the paraders sang. But on the way home, the band would try to lighten the mourners' grief by playing the brash and lively Negro jazz. So the white people got to hear it, liked it, and before long the jazz players had become popular entertainers. From New Orleans, the new music moved upriver to St. Louis, then Chicago, and eventually all over the world.

PARADES *don't always march to brass bands or martial music. In many places they're accompanied by folk music played on whatever instruments are available. Here a Swedish village celebrates a festival with a parade led by a sextet of violins.*

(SWEDISH NATL. TRAVEL OFFICE)

New Orleans was also the setting for a quaint "love story" connected with parade music. You'll remember that the Russian Grand Duke Alexis visited New Orleans in 1872, to take in the Mardi Gras. Well, as his first Carnival treat, the city officials escorted him to the theater to see a performance of a light opera entitled *Bluebeard.* In one act the show's star, Miss Lydia Thompson, sang a ballad called "If Ever I Cease to Love." The Grand Duke immediately fell madly in love with the song (or in love, some say, with the beautiful Miss Thompson). He applauded so heartily that she came back onstage several times afterward to sing encores of it.

The city officials escorting the Grand Duke nodded wisely to each other. Next day, when they staged the parade of King Rex for the royal visitor, they made sure that Miss Thompson was in the procession, riding a float and blowing kisses to the reviewing stand. They also made sure that every band in the parade played at least one chorus of "If Ever I Cease to Love." In consequence, the song has long outlived the Grand Duke. There *are* no more Russian grand dukes, but "If Ever I Cease to Love" is still the traditional accompaniment to the New Orleans Mardi Gras parade.

The words of the song, it's true, don't seem very fitting to a tumultuous street parade, but the lilting music is a pleasure to hear, even when rendered by brass bands and jazz bands. Just to give you some idea of the song that so enchanted the Grand Duke, here is a sample of the lyrics:

> "In a house, in a square, in a quadrant,
> In a street, in a lane, in a road,
> Turn to the left on the right hand,
> You see there my true love's abode.
> I go there a-courting and cooing,
> To my love like a dove,
> And swearing on my bended knee,
> If ever I cease to love,
> May the moon be turned into green cheese,
> If ever I cease to love . . ."

IX

The Slow Farewell

SOME OF THE MOST DAZZLING and resplendent parades ever held have been of the kind that no one really enjoys either marching in or watching—namely, the funeral procession that escorts a dead person to his or her last resting place.

All through history, man has tried to show how highly he thought of a lost loved one—and has tried to ease his own grief at the loss—by making that farewell gesture as reverent and affectionate as he could. Even before history began, as we know from evidence found at Stone Age gravesites, primitive man tried clumsily to make the departed one's last journey as easeful as possible. When a dead man was taken to the burying ground, his survivors also took along food, water, and his personal weapons, to be buried with him in case he should ever have need of them.

Nowadays, even poor people who can ill afford it will often go into debt to provide a lavish funeral for a dead relative. It may, in fact, be a far more elegant occasion than any outing that person ever enjoyed while he was alive. But it is only very recently that this ostentatious sort of funeral has become a custom among common folk. From the days of ancient Egypt down to the mid-nineteenth century, most ordinary people said their last good-byes in a simple and quiet family ceremony. The sumptuous public funeral was only for royalty, national heroes, and the richer classes, and any commoner who tried to imitate it would have been scorned as an impudent upstart.

No Egyptian peasant of 2500 B.C. would have dared hope for a fu-

AN EGYPTIAN PHARAOH *rides to his last resting place in a water-borne funeral procession on the River Nile, accompanied by nobles, priests, guards, slaves, and (in the bow of the first barge) weeping women.*

neral to match the pharaoh's. For one reason, the ancient Egyptians believed in a life after death, but they believed that everything in that afterlife would be the same as in this one. A pharaoh here would be a pharaoh over there, so he had to be buried with ceremonies befitting his high station, to make sure he'd be *recognized* as a pharaoh when he entered the other world. Since the miserable peasant was just going to be a peasant again over there, nobody (including himself) cared how he got buried.

What the pharaohs, nobles and wealthier Egyptians considered "fitting" burial ceremonies for themselves could hardly be called modest. They were so concerned about their mode of entrance into the next world that practically all of ancient Egypt's architectural and engineering skill went into the building of tombs. The three Great Pyramids at Gizeh, for example, were erected as tombs for the pharaohs Cheops, Khafre, and Menhaure. The interior of a tomb was furnished like a luxurious apartment for the living, and was decorated with paintings, carvings, and statuettes to keep the occupant entertained while he awaited his call to join the other world.

The funeral procession for a high-ranking personage would carry along food, wine, and tableware to stock the apartment for his stay there. They would also carry the best pieces of his jewelry, perfumes and lotions, his battle armor and weapons, to assure that he was well dressed and properly outfitted in the next life. His favorite horses might be killed on the spot and buried with him. Furthermore, not all of the mourners who marched out in the funeral parade would march home again. It was not uncommon for several of the dead man's servants, slaves, bodyguards, and even one or more of his wives to be sealed alive in the tomb with him.

Egypt was not the only civilization to practice this (to us) disgusting custom. The ancient Babylonians, Phoenicians, and others did it, too. The Sumerians would sometimes entomb as many as eighty slaves with a dead noble. But they mercifully put the slaves to death first, and then buried them in a crouching position, so they'd be ready to leap instantly to their feet as soon as their master needed them.

Eventually Greece displaced Egypt as the western world's loftiest example of civilization, and the Greeks were far *too* civilized to dream of burying live people with a dead one. Their sense of compassion was so highly developed, in fact, that they may be said to have invented the idea of paying tribute to an Unknown Soldier. After the Peloponnesian War, the city-state of Athens held an elaborate public funeral for the Athenian soldiers who had died in it. Because the thousands of dead had been buried on the battlefields where they fell, Athens ended its mass funeral with the ceremonial burial of an empty coffin to symbolize all of them.

A notable feature of ancient Greece's funeral practices is that there was a whole class of men who earned their living by hiring out to weep, wail, and sing mournful dirges during funeral processions. No young

THE EGYPTIAN FUNERAL PA-RADE's *destination was a tomb (sometimes inside a vast pyramid) furnished and decorated as richly as any palace for the living.*

(EGYPTIAN STATE TOURIST ADMIN.)

woman was ever allowed to march in such a procession, even if it
happened to be her husband's or child's funeral. Ancient Greece believed in male superiority, and women—at least young ones—were so
insignificant that they were barred from public functions. Only women
over sixty could join a funeral parade.

The Romans borrowed many of their funeral practices from Greece,
as they did so much else in their culture. For example, they adopted the
idea of having professional weepers and wailers for hire. But they
added some touches of their own. A Roman funeral wasn't entirely
solemn; the procession included capering buffoons and prank-playing
jesters who did their best to lighten the occasion by making both the
mourners and bystanders smile. One of the clowns would even be made-
up and costumed to resemble the dead man who was being buried—
perhaps in an attempt to demonstrate that *he* didn't feel too bad about
it. Farther along in the parade would come what the Romans called
"worthies": men wearing wax masks to look like the dead man. Their
job was to make known all the good deeds and heroic feats the man had
achieved during his lifetime, so they carried his various trophies or
acted-out his deeds in brief skits. After them would march ranks of
torchbearers, and then the man's family, friends, freedmen, and
slaves.

It was really a momentous event when a Roman emperor died. He
would be buried in the normal way, with a splendid funeral procession,
but then his courtiers would pretend to keep him alive for a while yet.
After Septimius Severus died and was buried, in the year A.D. 211, his

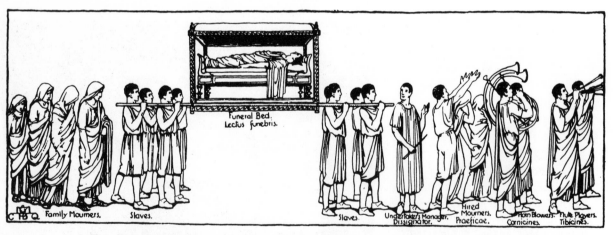

THE ROMAN FUNERAL *was actually much more spectacular than this old drawing indicates. This merely shows the order of march: at the front of the procession (right) were the musicians, then the hired mourners, the undertaker in
charge, the pallbearers carrying the funeral couch, and then the mourning
family.*

court attendants made a wax image of him and laid it on an ivory bed which was placed in the entranceway of his palace. For seven days, all the members of the Roman Senate sat on one side of the bed and all the women of the palace on the other. Every day, the court doctors came and examined the "patient," and every day they pronounced him a little sicker.

On the seventh day, when the doctors finally conceded that the emperor had died, four young senators and four cavalrymen belonging to the Equestrian Order took the bed on their shoulders and carried it to the Forum. There two choirs selected from Rome's noblest families, one of women and one of children, took turns singing hymns in honor of the dead Septimius. Then, followed by nearly every citizen of Rome, the ivory bed was carried outside the city walls, to a field where an immense, five-storey structure had been erected. The outside of it was decorated with golden draperies, mural tapestries, paintings and ivory carvings, but the inside was chock full of brushwood and kindling. The bed and its wax image were hoisted into the structure's second storey, and aromatic herbs and incense were heaped around them.

Next, the spectators were treated to an exhibition of riding skill, as all the horsemen of the Equestrian Order rode around and around the tower in wheeling, shifting, changing formations. They were followed by a company of charioteers giving a similar exhibition of precision driving. After that, the heir to the throne, the new Emperor Caracalla, took a torch and set it to the building. As the flames caught and roared up along the walls, a trap in the structure's fifth storey opened, and an eagle burst out of the blaze to soar away into the sky. This final touch was meant to symbolize Septimius's soul rising from earth to heaven, to dwell among the gods.

Although they tried to mask the sadness of a funeral with touches of high drama or low comedy, the Romans really felt it to be a quite dismal occasion, and so their traditional funeral colors were black and purple. These are still the colors of mourning in most of Europe and the Americas, but for a while in the early days of Christianity the gloomy colors were replaced with bright and joyous white. The Christians were following the custom of the Jews, who also believed in a new life after death and wore white at funerals as a token of that "newness." For the same reason, the people of China, Japan, and Korea still wear white for mourning. But other peoples have other ideas about what is the proper funeral color. The Egyptian Arabs prefer yellow, the Ethiopians gray, while the Syrians and Armenians drape their coffins with cloth of sky blue, to signify "heaven."

Various societies, too, have different views as to whether a funeral is

IN CHINA, *until quite recently, it was the custom for a whole "bodyguard" of soldiers on horses—all made of paper—to take part in a funeral procession. At the graveside they were burned, so their spirits would "accompany" the dead man to the next world.*

an occasion for reverent sadness or for outright fear. Long before the English poet John Donne wrote that "any man's death diminishes me," the Jews already believed that they should mourn at even a stranger's death. Their book of holy scriptures, the Torah, says that anyone who sees a funeral passing should join the procession and accompany it to the graveyard.

Quite the contrary, in parts of Portugal the people are so fearful of the presence of death that they think no one should "imitate" it by being asleep or even lying down when a funeral passes the door. These people will scamper to rouse anyone in the house who is abed, and some of them even run to the barn to prod the animals to their feet. The most fearfully superstitious of them won't stand on the shady side of a street to watch a funeral parade, because even that much darkness hints of the threat of death.

In other parts of Europe, it is the custom for the children to hold a mock funeral every New Year's Day. In places as far apart as the Isle of Guernsey, Austria, and Poland, the children of a village make a straw doll image of "Death," lay it in a wooden box for a coffin, and parade it solemnly down the main street. Then they either take it to an outlying field and burn it, or throw it into the nearest pond, while reciting a verse that goes something like this:

> "If we bore him not away,
> Death throughout the year would stay."

Everywhere in the world, funerals are customarily held in the daytime, because people feel that the occasion is dreary enough without adding to it the gloom of night. But there *have* been nighttime funerals. In the seventeenth century, the officials of the French government detested the playwright Molière because his comedies often made fun of them. So, when he died in 1673, the officials spitefully refused his family a permit for a daytime funeral. He had to be buried by night, but that didn't stop his thousands of admirers from turning out to join the procession. And indeed, with all those thousands of marchers carrying flaring torches. Molière's funeral was almost as well lighted as if it had been staged at midday.

Not all funerals have taken place on land, and not all burials in the ground. The Scandinavian Vikings of the eighth to tenth centuries lived out their lives as sea rovers and pirates, and would have been horrified to think of a dead Viking being buried anywhere but at sea. An ordinary sailor who died would merely be bundled into a shroud of furs, together with his battle weapons and shield, and slipped overboard—perhaps after his shipmates had held a short ceremony commending his soul to the care of their war god, Odin. But when a Viking chieftain died, the ritual was more spectacular—possibly the most fitting burial for a hero that has ever been devised.

The dragon-prowed "long ship" that he had captained was loaded with all his weapons, shields, and ornaments, plus enough food and

AT THIS FUNERAL *of a Moslem dignitary, his coffin is set on a trestle so the dead man can "review" a parade marching past in his honor.*

(FRENCH EMBASSY)

drink to sustain him on his voyage to Valhalla (the abode of the gods). His body was laid on a platform amidships and the sail was raised. Then the whole crew stepped ashore and let the unmanned ship drift away from the coast as the wind took it. When it had gone not quite out of bowshot, the crewmen raised their bows and shot fire-tipped arrows at the ship until it caught ablaze. It burned slowly down to the water-line, slowly careened, and then suddenly plunged to the bottom.

The highest Scandinavian rulers, though, were given a sort of combination sea-and-land funeral when they died. A king's body would be laid with all his belongings and treasures in one of the long ships, and then this great vessel would be transported several miles inland for burial. That must have been a funeral procession worth seeing. Some of the long ships measured more than a hundred feet and weighed at least that many tons. The transporting would have been done by innumerable men hauling on ropes, while other men wedged log rollers under the ship's bows, retrieved them at the stern when the ship had rolled over them, and hurried them up to the bows again. The work of digging a grave big enough for one of these vessels must have required another small army of laborers.

Incidentally, archaeologists have dug up one of these funeral ships in Norway and found that the bones of the buried ruler are those of a female. They're still a little puzzled as to how a woman managed to rule such an intensely masculine and warlike society—and how she came to deserve a hero's burial.

THIS VIKING "LONG SHIP" *was hauled overland and buried in the Norway earth about a thousand years ago. Dug up in this century, it was found to have been the "coffin" of a Viking queen. A female slave and all the queen's prized possessions had been buried with her.*

(N.Y. PUBLIC LIBRARY)

Other heroes have had stranger modes of progress to their last rest. The warrior called El Cid Campeador ("the lord champion") was Spain's hero in the eleventh-century war against the Moorish invaders. The Moors were so terrified of El Cid that, when he was finally killed in battle, his men tied his body upright in his saddle and sent the dead Cid galloping ahead of them in a fresh attack. The Moors broke and fled at the sight of him, and that battle was won for Spain. Afterward, the Spanish soldiers formed a funeral procession and led El Cid, still strapped to his horse but now clad in luxurious robes, halfway across the country—so that every Spaniard could pay homage to him—before he was buried at last.

When England's King Henry V died in France in 1422, his courtiers naturally wanted his body transported home to England for the proper royal burial. But in those days there was no way known to embalm or preserve a corpse to last during a long trip. So King Henry's body was boiled down to the bones, and just his skeleton was sent home to London for the funeral. In 1805, when the British admiral, Lord Horatio Nelson, was killed while defeating Napoleon's fleet in the sea battle of Trafalgar (near the Rock of Gibraltar), his under-officers managed to transport his body back to England by preserving it in a cask of rum.

London paid tribute to Nelson with a tremendous funeral procession. The coffin in which he was buried at St. Paul's Cathedral was carved from the mainmast of one of the French ships he had vanquished. The funeral carriage was a small-scale model of the flagship H.M.S. *Victory* which he had commanded, and the ship's crewmen served as his pall-bearers.

THE FUNERAL CAR *of Admiral Nelson was designed in the shape of his flagship, the* Victory. *His coffin (under the canopy) was carved from the mainmast of a French warship he had captured.*

For the London funeral of the "Iron Duke" of Wellington, the British general who defeated Napoleon at Waterloo, the carriage that bore his coffin was made of solid bronze, cast from the melted-down French cannons that the British had captured. The carriage was twenty feet long, seventeen feet high, and weighed eighteen tons. It required six wheels to support its weight, twelve horses to pull it, and had built-in machinery to lower its canopy in order for the carriage to squeeze through Temple Arch. (The historian Thomas Carlyle, who watched the funeral parade, called the funeral car "of all objects I ever saw, the abominably ugliest," but Queen Victoria, who rode in the procession, thought the carriage "a beautiful sight.")

A funeral procession, like almost every other sort of parade, has occasionally made a contribution to history. When Great Britain's King Edward VII died in 1910, there marched in his funeral procession the royal rulers of nine nations and royal representatives of three others. In addition to the new King George V of Britain, there were Kaiser Wilhelm II of Germany, Czar Ferdinand of Bulgaria, the kings of Spain, Portugal, Denmark, Greece, Norway, and Belgium, Archduke Franz Ferdinand of Austria-Hungary, Italy's Duke of Aosta, and Grand Duke Michael of Russia.

This company of royalty marched partly as a show of respect to the departed monarch, but not entirely for that reason. At that time, many countries in the world were undergoing a ferment of political unrest. Their people were getting tired of being ruled by royal families who governed by "divine right," and were making sullen gestures of rebellion. The royal rulers' get-together at King Edward's funeral was their own gesture of solidarity, to show the world that they stood united against any threats of social change. But it was really rather a pathetic last stand. The changes did come. Of the twelve nations represented by royalty at that 1910 funeral, eight are now governed either by elected presidents or non-royal dictators—Spain, Portugal, Italy, Russia, Germany, Bulgaria, Austria, and Hungary (these last have split from one nation into two since then).

Two other funerals, in our own time, are destined to be remembered in history books forever. The first took place on November 25, 1963, when John F. Kennedy, the thirty-fifth President of the United States— and the fourth to die by an assassin's bullet—was laid to rest in the Arlington National Cemetery.

The funeral of a dead President, since he was also Commander-in-Chief of the nation's armed forces, is a military funeral and follows all the age-old customs of military burial. It is as well that these traditions existed to help direct the organization of President Kennedy's funeral,

because his sudden, tragic death had shocked into numbness almost
everyone concerned with it. As evidence, photographs of the procession
show the leaders of the world's nations marching behind his coffin, not
in any formal order, but in a shuffling, straggling bunch. Bowed down
by the grief and despair of the occasion, no emperor or president cared
to fret about the "proper" order of precedence or any show of his own
pomp and importance.

On that Monday morning, President Kennedy's coffin was removed
from the rotunda of the Capitol building, where it had lain in state the
day before. Nine honor-guard pallbearers from the several services—
Army, Navy, Marines, Air Force, and Coast Guard—carried it down
the long flight of Capitol steps and placed it gently on a caisson. This is
a plain and unadorned, four-wheeled carriage of a sort that in oldtime
wars carried the ammunition for an army's artillery.

The caisson was drawn by six pairs of matched gray horses, and, in
keeping with an old military tradition, the six right-side horses wore
empty saddles. Behind the caisson, a soldier led a black horse, also
wearing an empty saddle. From it hung a sheathed sword and in the
saddle stirrups were cavalry boots—but reversed, pointing backward,
as a sign that the warrior would never mount again. This custom dates
back at least nine hundred years, to the army of Genghis Khan.

At the White House, President Kennedy's widow, Jacqueline, and his
brothers, Robert and Edward, decided to walk behind the caisson—
instead of riding in the limousines prepared for them—as the procession made its way to St. Matthew's Cathedral. Also afoot in the parade
were Lyndon Johnson, the new President of the United States; the
Presidents of France, Ireland, South Korea, and the Philippines; the
Emperor of Ethiopia; the First Deputy Premier of the Soviet Union;
Prince Philip and the Prime Minister of Britain; the Chancellor of

Germany, and heads of state or high-ranking emissaries from practically every other country in the world.

After the funeral Mass at the cathedral, Mrs. Kennedy, the other members of the family and all the visiting dignitaries rode in limousines behind the caisson as the six gray horses drew it out of Washington and across the Potomac River to Arlington, Virginia. The procession was three miles long. All the military troops in the parade—and there were contingents from other countries as well as from all the American services—carried their rifles reversed: muzzles down, stocks upward. Muffled drums beat the slow, slow cadence of the Dead March, while the British Army's Black Watch bagpipers played a mournful dirge. The procession took more than an hour to reach the cemetery.

During the graveside ceremonies, the U. S. Army's "Revolutionary War" Fife and Drum Corps paraded, the Irish Guards performed a funeral drill, a flight of fifty jet fighters roared across the sky, and the President's private plane, Air Force One, dipped its wings in salute as it flew over.

After the coffin had been lowered into the ground, the honor guard folded and presented to Mrs. Kennedy the American flag that had covered it for three days. There were final prayers, a troop of soldiers fired a rifle volley and a bugler blew "Taps," that most heart-touching of all bugle calls. Then Mrs. Kennedy stepped forward to light an "eternal flame" at the grave. The funeral was over, then. The flame still burns.

Just fourteen months later, on January 30, 1965, the world joined in mourning Sir Winston Churchill, probably the greatest statesman of this century and certainly the most universally beloved. There were no hurried preparations for this funeral, as there had been for President Kennedy's. Sir Winston was ninety years old, and had been critically ill for nearly two weeks before he finally succumbed; rehearsals for the ceremonies had quietly been held during that time. In any case, there was no indecision about the arrangements for his funeral. Sir Winston had dictated many of the details himself, several years earlier. (He particularly wanted plenty of military bands.)

Several observers commented that this procession was the most splendid since the Duke of Wellington's funeral in 1852, but it is hard to imagine that Wellington's could have been any grander. And it's sure to be a long, long time before any other man deserves or gets such a pageant as accompanied Sir Winston's last march. This funeral surpassed even President Kennedy's in the number of spectators. It has been estimated that 350 million people—more than one-sixth of all the people on earth—saw either the direct telecasts or re-plays of the TV films and tapes.

That Saturday morning, eight uniformed but bareheaded Grenadier Guardsmen carried Sir Winston's coffin out of Westminster Hall, where it had been visited by more than 300,000 Englishmen while it lay in state. The grenadiers lifted the coffin onto an empty gun carriage, then put on their tall bearskin hats to march beside it. The coffin was made of lead and weighed five hundred pounds. (To make sure that it wouldn't overtax the pallbearers, an even heavier coffin had been carried during the rehearsals.) The coffin was covered with the Union Jack, and on top of the flag was a black velvet cushion on which lay the medals and ribbons marking Sir Winston as a Knight of the Order of the Garter.

At Churchill's own request, the carriage on which his coffin rode was pulled, not by horses, but by a crew of Royal Navy "ratings" (enlisted sailors, not officers). Before he was Prime Minister of Britain, Churchill had twice served as First Lord of the Admiralty, so it was no surprise that he wanted his last parade to have a naval air to it. The sailors marched in eight columns. Each two columns hauled on a white rope between them that was attached to the gun carriage. As they towed the carriage out of New Palace Yard, the honor guard fell into place. These were soldiers of the Irish Guard and a detachment of very young cadets from Harrow, Sir Winston's boyhood school.

The mile-long procession set out from Westminster Hall when Big Ben, the great-voiced bell in the Parliament clock tower, tolled 9:45 a.m. After that moment the bell was silenced, not to strike again that day. Toward the head of the procession rode Lady Churchill, her son Randolph, and daughters Mary and Sarah, in a horse-drawn carriage driven by a coachman in red jacket and gold-braided top hat.

WINSTON CHURCHILL'S COF-FIN, *on a gun carriage drawn by marching sailors and accompanied by a guard of Grenadiers, leaves St. Paul's Cathedral after the funeral ceremony.*
(WIDE WORLD PHOTOS)

There were lancers, hussars, and dragoons—bearskin hats, gleaming helmets, plumes of white and red. There were the State Trumpeters in Elizabethan costumes. There were the mounted troopers of the Household Cavalry, wearing gold helmets and scarlet coats, and carrying bared sabers. The Household Cavalry's drum horse (named Alexander the Great) carried two huge silver kettledrums, symbolically silent on this occasion, though there were many other drums in the various bands to beat out the Dead March. At this pace, the parade took an hour to cover the two-mile route along Whitehall, through Trafalgar Square, along The Strand and Fleet Street, and finally up Ludgate Hill (where workmen spread sand on the icy incline so the horses wouldn't slip).

The entire route between Westminster and St. Paul's Cathedral was lined with Royal Marines and London policemen, stationed alternately, and with the close-packed crowds of people who had traveled here from all over the Isles to pay their last tribute to Sir Winston. Some of them wept, but none cheered. The parade passed through a respectful hush, broken only by the thump . . . thump of the drums, the dirges of bands and pipers, and the hoofbeats of the horses.

At St. Paul's, Sir Winston's dearest friends and most notable mourners were waiting. Queen Elizabeth was there, and this was the first time in English history that a reigning monarch had ever waited upon a commoner at a public affair. Prince Philip, the rest of the royal family, Prime Minister Harold Wilson and all the other high officials of the British government were there. So were four kings—Frederik IX of Denmark, Olav V of Norway, Baudouin of Belgium, and Constantine of Greece. So were Queen Juliana and Prince Bernhard of the Netherlands, Grand Duke Jean of Luxembourg, the Presidents of France, Iceland, Israel and Uruguay, former U. S. President Dwight Eisenhower, the former Premier of Japan, the Prime Ministers of Canada, Australia, New Zealand, Malta, and Rhodesia, the Premiers of Finland, the Congo, South Korea, and Sweden, a Deputy Premier of the Soviet Union, the Chancellor of Germany, the Foreign Ministers of Argentina and India, and lesser dignitaries from eighty-five other countries.

When the eight grenadiers carried Sir Winston's coffin into the cathedral, there marched before them a troop of heralds in antique costumes of red, gold, and blue silk. The heralds carried the banners of Churchill's family, a shield bearing his coat-of-arms, his sword and spurs of knighthood, and black velvet pillows on which reposed the medals he had received from a score of countries.

After the funeral service, when the grenadiers carried the coffin out of the cathedral, they were followed by Queen Elizabeth and all the other heads of state, who gave Sir Winston one last affectionate salute as the sailors hauled on their ropes and the procession got underway again. Now it was only a short march to the Tower of London, where the parade was met with a salute from the massed Yeoman Warders of the Tower (the "Beefeaters"), dressed in their medieval costumes and "presenting arms" with antique pikestaffs.

The last lap of Sir Winston's journey was to be by train from Waterloo Station—on the other side of the Thames River—to the village of Bladon, where he would be buried outside the walls of the Churchills' ancestral Blenheim Palace. But it was by water, now, that he made the crossing from the Tower to the pier near the railroad station.

A launch was waiting at the Tower, and his coffin was lifted aboard. Churchill's widow, son and daughters, and the grenadier pallbearers also stepped on board the launch, but the rest of the parade stayed ashore. As the launch moved away from the dock, the old-fashioned cannons of the Honorable Artillery Company boomed a nineteen-gun salute from the embankment, and four Royal Air Force jet fighters flashed past, just a couple of hundred feet overhead.

The launch and a few small accompanying boats turned upstream— and at this moment, as a reporter wrote later, "there came a tribute so slow and majestic that it might almost have been missed." The banks of the Thames are lined with wharves and dockyards, each marked by its towering steam crane. As the launch bearing Sir Winston's body passed, all of these massive machines—like great prehistoric beasts, or perhaps like England's legendary giants, Gog and Magog—silently, ponderously, slowly bowed down to him in farewell.

Bibliographical Note

As far as I can discover, this is the first book ever written specifically on the subject of parades: their infinite variety, their history, lore, technique and mystique. This is surprising, considering that the parade is an age-old, worldwide and everyday occurrence. The present work was compiled in part from conversations and correspondence with natives in or of the various countries mentioned in the text, partly from my own travels and observations, and in largest part from a wide reading in all kinds of books: histories, geographies, military manuals, tourist guides, travelers' memoirs, and mountains of Chamber of Commerce-type literature. A bibliography of all this material would probably run to book length itself, and still would not provide any practical catalog of "further reading" in the subject. The short list here cites a few books that were of especial help to me, though only two of them really have anything to do with parades *per se*. They are C. P. Fox's fondly nostalgic *Circus Parades* and L. F. Vaughn's *Parade and Float Guide*, which offers expert information on how to organize, equip, and direct a community parade.

BATES, E. W. *Pageants and Pageantry*. Boston: Ginn, 1912.

BOATNER, MARK, III. *Military Customs and Traditions*. New York: McKay, 1956.

BRAND, JOHN. *Observations on Popular Antiquities*. London: Chatto & Windus, 1877.

BREDON, JULIET, AND MITROPHANOV, IGOR. *The Moon Year; a Record of Chinese Customs and Festivals*. Shanghai: Kelly & Walsh, 1927.

CHAILLEY, JACQUES. *40,000 Years of Music*. New York: Farrar, Straus & Giroux, 1964.

CHAMBERS, R., ed. *The Book of Days*. Vol. I, II. Philadelphia: Lippincott, 1863-64.

DOUGLAS, GEORGE WILLIAM. *The American Book of Days*. Rev. by Helen Douglas Compton. New York: Wilson, 1948.

EBERHARD, WOLFRAM. *Chinese Festivals*. New York: Schuman, 1952.

FLETCHER, I. K. *Splendid Occasions in English History: 1520-1947*. London: Cassell, 1951.

FOWLER, W. W. *The Roman Festivals of the Period of the Republic*. London: Macmillan, 1899.

Fox, Charles Philip. *Circus Parade*. Watkins Glen, N. Y.: Century House, 1953.

Gaster, Theodor. *New Year: Its History, Customs and Superstitions*. New York: Abelard-Schuman, 1955.

Harrison, F., and Rimmer, J. *European Musical Instruments*. London: Studio Vista, 1964.

Harrison, Jane. *Ancient Art and Ritual*. London: Butterworth, 1927.

Hone, William. *The Every-Day Book; or, The Guide to the Year*. London: Tegg, 1826.

Hone, William. *The Table Book of Daily Recreation and Information*. London: Tegg, ca. 1830.

Hone, William. *The Year Book of Daily Recreation and Information*. London: Tegg, 1832.

Ickis, Marguerite. *The Book of Festival Holidays*. New York: Dodd, Mead, 1964.

Laurie, W. F. B. *The Idol-Shrine*. London: Smith, Elder, 1851.

Lyman, Susan E. *The Story of New York*. New York: Crown, 1964.

Murray, Marian. *Circus!* New York: Appleton-Century-Crofts, 1956.

Pemberton, J. L., and Laver, James. *Royal Progress*. London: Collins, 1955.

Petrides, Anne. *State Barges on the Thames*. London: Evelyn, 1959.

Spicer, Dorothy G. *Festivals of Western Europe*. New York: Wilson, 1958.

Still, Bayrd. *Mirror for Gotham*. New York: New York University Press, 1956.

Urlin, Ethel L. *Festivals, Holy Days, and Saints' Days*. London: Simpkin, Marshall, 1915.

Vaughn, L. F. *Vaughn's Parade and Float Guide*. Minneapolis: Denison, 1956.

Walsh, William S. *Curiosities of Popular Customs*. Philadelphia: Lippincott, 1897.

Withington, Robert. *English Pageantry: An Historical Outline*. Vol. I, II. Cambridge, Mass.: Harvard University Press, 1918-20.

Workman, B. K. *They Saw It Happen in Classical Times*. New York: Barnes & Noble, 1964.

Index